Holding Grief

holding grief

*a love letter
from a recovering
death denier*

jennifer elliott

Holding Grief: A Love Letter from a Recovering Death Denier

Jennifer Elliott Consulting, INC, Bend, OR
© 2024 by Jennifer Elliott

This is a work of nonfiction. Nonetheless, some names of locations, some names of people, and some identifying details and personal characteristics of the individuals involved have been changed. In addition, certain people who appear in these pages are composites of a number of individuals and their experiences.

Cover illustration by Jason Booher.
Author photo by Gallivan Photo.
Book design by Vinnie Kinsella.

ISBN 979-8-9902369-0-5 (hardback)
ISBN 979-8-9902369-1-2 (paperback)
ISBN 979-8-9902369-2-9 (ebook)

Library of Congress Control Number: 2024905827

For Tim

Note for the Reader

These stories were written and printed in linear order, from my first memory of grief to the most recent. My age has been noted at the top of each chapter to provide a frame of reference.

Like cloud formations, memories are dynamic. We each bring our own state of mind, perceptions, beliefs, sensibilities, points of view, prejudices, and sense of time to our memories. As a result, when people share an experience, we each will have our own unique version of the same experience. The stories you are about to read are true as I remember them. Some names and locations have been changed to protect identities.

Table of Contents

Introduction

"Jerry is getting close," said the hospice nurse, listening to his fading heartbeat with the stethoscope. My mom and I were sitting on the couch nearby and immediately jumped to our feet, moving to stand one on each side of him. His breath slowed. There were long pauses between each one, and then there were no more.

This was the first time I had ever been with someone when they died. In the months and years that followed, I experienced what I now refer to as "a shift." I started changing. Perhaps it was a midlife crisis? Since I was middle age, it made sense that it would be. And in the five years leading up to Jerry's death, there had been four deaths, in close succession, in our family. I was thinking a lot about death. And grief. Being in the presence of Jerry, my mom's partner, as he took his last breath — put it in the forefront. I always look back at this moment as the point of origin of this shift. I set out on a quest to understand what I was feeling and how it was affecting my well-being. I began to explore.

Whether we know it or not, we have a relationship with not only people in our lives but also with circumstances. We are taught how to respond to these circumstances by our families, our peer groups, and our culture. They are taught or learned, explicitly, implicitly, or sometimes surreptitiously. An association is now formed with these circumstances. We have a relationship with food. We have a relationship with our bodies. We have a relationship with money. We have a relationship with time. We also have relationships with change, sex, adversity, illness, even the weather, and finally, we have a relationship with death. We have a relationship with both our own death and the way the deaths of others affect us, in particular through grief.

The acquaintance I had with death, and grief — it was estranged. I saw this relationship as being like an affiliation with a second cousin whom I only very rarely saw at weddings or reunions. She would perhaps live far away in a state I have never visited. This state would have tornadoes, and when I heard about a tornado touching down there, I thought about that second cousin in a fleeting sort of way. It seemed I had lived nearly half a century so preoccupied with my own busyness that I somehow had this idea that death had not really touched me.

Or had it, and it was just that I hadn't given it the attention it demanded?

Introduction

The journey continued. Before I could really understand this connection I had with death and grief, I had to get an understanding of its origin in my life. I began to retrace all the times death had crossed my path, beginning with my very first memory of mortality — I didn't just want to have a memory of it but remember what it had felt like. And what I became aware of was that not only was death not estranged from me, but in some instances, death had bumped into me like a passenger standing too close on a New York subway. And this happened much more frequently than I had realized. But it was a forced relationship. Death was doing all the pursuing, stalking me relentlessly, especially in my later years. It pointed to only one verdict. I found myself guilty.

I had become a bona fide death denier.

Elizabeth Kubler-Ross, the author of the groundbreaking book *On Death and Dying*, was the first to name denial as one of the five stages of grief for those who are terminally ill. In an effort to protect ourselves at such a time, we simply deny we are dying; denial is a defense mechanism with which we simply reject something as untrue. Subsequently, the author and anthropologist Ernest Becker, whose book *The Denial of Death* won the Pulitzer Prize in 1974, would go on to suggest that our very character is shaped around the denial of our own mortality. It remains unclear where the term *death denial* came from, but we can look to both Kubler-Ross and Becker as starting the conversation.

What is a death denier? They are actually quite common in the United States, where we are an age-fearing culture and where many live life as though we will never die, and those around us won't die either. Somehow along the way, we have grown to believe, or like to believe, we are immune to death. It lingers on the outskirts, only in the periphery. We don't see it. It only happens in hospitals behind closed doors or somewhere else out of sight. We hide it. We hide from it. We don't talk about it, or if we do, it's in whispers. We don't teach about it. And I daresay, sometimes we are even ashamed when it happens to someone in our family. It's taboo. It's too painful. It hurts too much. When it does happen, we are caught off guard. Because we deny it, we run from it.

Closely associated with death-denying is unresolved grief. Here is what I know about unresolved grief. It follows you. No matter where you are or where you are going, it is going with you. You can try to run from it. You can try to hide in a booth at a restaurant, but soon you will look up and see it staring at you from the counter. It doesn't care if you ignore it; it has no ego. Grief will chew you up, swallow you whole, and spit you back out. It will hunt you down. It will creep up on you. It will surprise you. Like a toddler (and even some full-grown adults), unresolved grief doesn't care if you give it positive attention or negative attention — it just wants attention.

This brings me to the next point. You must give it attention. To heal, to resolve the grief, you must do the work. This begs the question, if you did give death and grief the proper attention, could you develop a better relationship with them? What if you were willing to talk about this uncomfortable topic and have those unwelcome conversations? What if you could go toe to toe with them and learn to accept them as part of your life, then take their hands and walk comfortably with them?

Courage. Willingness. Acceptance.

More questions still: Is there a right way to grieve? Is there a wrong way to grieve? Is there a better way to grieve? What do courage, willingness, and acceptance in the face of death and grief look like? If we did those things, could we expedite the grief work and healing process to go on to live freely and even fruitfully?

Recently, a friend asked me what I had been up to. I told her that I was writing a book about grief associated with death.

"Oh," she said. "So you're writing about bereavement."

How was it that I was eight chapters into writing this book and the word *bereavement* had never even occurred to me? Why hadn't it occurred to me? When I think about bereavement or the bereaved, I think of an old widow with gray hair who has just lost her husband.

They'd been married for sixty-two years. I can even picture her in my mind. She is wearing all black, a skirt with black nylons, and black, low-heeled pumps. She is sipping tea and eating pumpkin bread. While she had known her husband's death was coming, the widow feels terrible loneliness. The house is quiet. She misses his laugh and his squeeze of her hand. She thinks, *I'm afraid. I miss you. Life isn't the same now that you are gone.* She feels the raw pain, the sadness, and the emptiness of bereavement, of grief associated with death.

Somehow the word *bereaved* just doesn't say the same thing to me as *grief associated with death*. It's a label that names and identifies someone who is deprived of their loved one, but the feeling and the loss associated with the word feels insufficient in depth. It feels less personal. It feels idle. By using it, I had allowed it to hold me at a distance from the reality of death. The word *death* is uncomfortable but wakes me up to the rawness. And yet, bereaved is the word that is universal and known to all. Those who lost a family member to COVID are bereaved. The parents who lost their child in a car accident are bereaved. The daughter who lost her mother to cancer is bereaved. The soldier who lost a fellow soldier in combat is bereaved. The community that lost their children and teachers in a school shooting is bereaved. And yes, the elderly woman who lost her husband to old age is also bereaved. But by using that word, do we give ourselves permission to separate ourselves from those people? We can only imagine the raw pain, the sadness, the emptiness they feel for their loved ones. *Bereaved* is a polite summary of a rough, intimate experience.

The following remembrances are explorations into my experiences with the grief associated with death. Not all of them, but most of them. As I started writing, I was startled both by what I remembered and what I didn't remember. I started noticing threads of what had helped and facilitated the healing and what hadn't. I am not an authority on the subject of death or grief. I have no degrees in psychotherapy or grief counseling, but I am experienced in the subject.

If you reflect on the story of your life, you too are probably more experienced with death and grief than you may have thought. I make no promises to fix the pain you are feeling, but perhaps I can suggest ways in which to make the experience a better one.

Chapter 1

Feebee

8 years old

Our family had just moved to a new home in Dollar Point, nestled in the tall ponderosas on the northwest shore of Lake Tahoe. The house was single-story but for the studio above the garage. The four hallways formed a perfect square, with the laundry room in the middle. My room was located at one of the corners.

I loved my room. It had a built-in desk and drawers on one side, and on the other side, the wall was covered floor to ceiling with corkboard. I had a lot of fun decorating that corkboard. My mom loved antiques and had sprinkled them throughout the house. I used an antique brass bed, and Mom covered it with a big, navy-blue, velvety quilt. It was different from most brass beds because it did not have rounded corners or scrolly details. It was squarish and boxy. The headboard and footboard were held together with spindle-like columns, but the crests on top were square. The best part of the square crests was that they made the perfect balance beam. While I wasn't a gymnast, I loved to pretend I was. I would walk across the brass balance beam, dipping my toes down before each step, pretending to be Nadia Comaneci. And when I decided I'd had enough, I could do a free-fall on the bed.

I was in second grade when we moved into our new house, and soon after we settled in, I begged my mom for a kitten. She finally acquiesced when I told her the neighbor on Observation Drive had a pregnant cat and I would get first pick of the litter. I chose the largest all-white male kitten; he had one blue eye and one green eye. I named the cat after a horse who lived up the street from some good friends who lived in Olympic Valley. You couldn't have horses in Dollar Point, but you could in Olympic Valley. I thought it was cool that they had a horse pastured right outside their house. The horse was named Feebee. Right then and there when I met that horse, I decided my first pet, whatever its species, would be called Feebee.

In my life now, I give a lot of thought to naming my pets. You have to practice it. You call it out a few times, make sure the name suits its personality. I have two regrets about my first cat; the first regret is naming him Feebee — a terrible choice for this particular cat. It still bothers me, and it's even hard to write it. Despite all that, his name didn't seem to bother him.

That cat and I were good buddies. He slept on my

bed and shed his white fur all over the navy-blue, velvety quilt. I fed him, and I was his personal valet. He was an efficient hunter. His very favorite activity, above all others, was exploring the attic. The entrance to the attic was in the ceiling right outside my bedroom. We had eight-foot ceilings in that house, so to get up into the attic, my dad would bring the six-foot ladder, and then we would have to lift ourselves in through the small square hole.

My dad owned a lumberyard. He brought home cut pieces of plywood for the attic and laid them on top of the bright-pink insulation, which looked like cotton candy. Whenever we went into the attic, Dad always reminded me, "Don't touch the insulation. It has shards of glass in it. It will cut you." It seemed weird that they would manufacture something that looked just like cotton candy but couldn't be touched. It looked so soft and fluffy and inviting, like a pink stuffed toy. It was the same color of pink my grandma Trudi wore on her fingernails. I always wished I could touch it.

On top of the plywood, we stored old receipts and taxes along with Christmas ornaments and Easter decorations. We didn't need to get into the attic very often, but when we did, Feebee came too. He would climb up the ladder and leap into the attic. He would be up there for hours, smelling, sniffing, exploring, hunting. My dad would climb up there, pull down what was needed, and then leave the attic open and the ladder in place so that the cat could come back down when he was ready.

It must have been Easter because I remember the snow was melting. My mom and dad set up the ladder. Feebee just lay down at the base. My mom and dad pulled the boxes out, and my dad, thinking the cat might still want adventure, left the attic door open and the ladder in place. Feebee just lay there, looking up at the ladder and the square hole in the ceiling.

"He's completely listless," murmured my dad under his breath.

That was the first time I had ever heard the word *listless*. Feebee was indeed listless, lacking energy or enthusiasm. This was particularly noteworthy in this instance, as he was being presented with his favorite activity of all time. I recall there being some discussion between my mom and dad that I wasn't necessarily being kept from but wasn't privy to either. It was about the vet and the cat and how best to coordinate their schedules.

It may have been the next day or in the days that followed, my dad came into my bedroom. I had been playing on my brass bed again and could tell by the look on his face something was wrong. I immediately sat on the footboard, which wasn't comfortable because the square crests cut into my legs. He told me that Feebee had been sick. He had had feline leukemia, a kind of cat cancer, and had been put down. My dad hugged me tight. I was sad, as I would have liked the opportunity to say goodbye to him.[1] My second regret.

I remember the crests of the footboard pinching my thighs. I remember this uncomfortable feeling in my stomach and an ache in my heart. It felt empty in a way that I had never felt before. And my eyes began stinging. And then I remember looking at the navy-blue, velvety quilt. He wouldn't be there to take naps. He wouldn't shed on it anymore. He was gone.

Most sympathy cards say, "We are so sorry for your loss." *Loss* seems to be the word most often associated with grief. And in some cases, it's fitting, particularly with those incidents associated with grief but not grief associated with death. If you lose your job, you can

---

1. I'm not sure if my parents thought that telling me later would somehow protect me from the pain and sadness or if this was just a product of the time. And I wonder if it occurred to veterinarians back then to invite families to be a part of their pet's death. In the 1970s, animals and pets didn't seem to have the same level of membership in the family that they do now. I don't remember ever seeing people bringing their pets on airplanes, or into restaurants or grocery stores, or to their jobs. There was no pet health insurance available. Pets have a much higher status in our lives today than they did fifty years ago. So, with that in mind, it would make sense that a vet would just take care of it.

replace it with a new one. If you lose your keys, they might turn up again. If you lose money, you can typically make more. When I think of the word *loss*, I think of it being used about something that is replaceable. If I think of the word *empty*, I think of it as being refillable. But when a person or a pet dies, they are gone. No one and no single thing can ever fill that space or void that they have left behind. When Feebee died, it was the first time I truly experienced "goneness."

If someone or something is gone, they are no longer present, and when I add the suffix *-ness*, they are in a state of being gone, which will not change. They will perpetually be gone, with no chance of returning. *Goneness*, noun. But while this person or thing is now gone — the void that is left, the absence — *is* a form of existence. The void is not a void. In fact, the negative space *is* a space, in the same way that, when a puzzle piece is removed from a puzzle, the only thing that will make the puzzle whole again is to fill it with a piece of the exact shape, size, and color, in other words to use *the* puzzle piece that was previously there. When people speak of repressing grief, it means they either are not acknowledging or are simply ignoring this most unwelcome and uncomfortable presence.

But it is real.

It is there.

Chapter 2

Jimmy

13 years old

The space between elementary school and high school is sometimes called middle school and sometimes called junior high. I'm embarrassed to admit that despite having been an educator for over thirty years, I still don't really know the difference. I just know that for the student, it is an awkward time, which can often feel like purgatory.

Do you remember your middle school math teacher — any of them? What can you tell me about them? In detail.

As I work in education, I feel I have some small bit of authority to tell you this: There are specific types of both middle school and high school math teachers, and they each fall into one of these categories:

A. They like kids but aren't good at teaching math.
B. They are good at teaching math but don't like kids.

C. They like kids AND are good at teaching math.

D. They don't like kids and aren't good at teaching math.

Now think again about your middle school math teacher experiences. How would you score those teachers? Whether or not you'd like to admit it, they may quite possibly have affected the trajectory of your life or profession. They did mine.

In seventh grade, first period, I had Mr. Barney Wilen. I can't tell you a single smidgen about my sixth-grade math teacher. Not. One. Single. Thing. I don't remember the person — male or female. I don't remember the classroom. Nothing. Completely blank. It's sort of liberating, actually. But Mr. Wilen was in category C. He liked kids, *and* he was good at teaching math, which in the world of middle school (or high school) math teachers is like hitting the daily double. He wore glasses and cardigan sweaters. He had a big nose and reminded me of my grandpa. He was funny. Not only was I successful in his class, but I *felt* successful in his class.

More than math, what I remember about Mr. Wilen's class was Current Events. Every first period, one of us (one at a time, assigned a different day) had to share a current event. It forced us to either watch the news or read the paper (remember that this was long before the internet or social media). Mr. Wilen knew this, and that was the point.

It was during my seventh-grade year that both John Lennon's murder and President Ronald Reagan's assassination attempt happened. Warren Mochinski told us in Current Events that John Lennon had been shot. I can't remember which classmate told us that President Reagan had been shot because the afternoon before, during seventh-grade English, sixth period, Mrs. K. — in tears — had already told us. In truth, at the time, I didn't understand the gravity of what this all meant. I find it interesting that it was deaths, or a brush with death, that I remember from Current Events.

Because of all the success I experienced in Mr. Wilen's seventh-grade math class, I was catapulted into Ms. Glower's eighth-grade advanced math class. My older brother had Ms. Glower two years earlier. I remember a lot of conversations around the dinner table and him airing his grievances about his experience with her. It was difficult not to have a preconceived notion of how this would unfold. As it turned out, I was indeed in over my head.

Here is what I remember. Ms. Glower seemed to be over fifty, but I can't say for sure because teachers you don't like when you're in middle school always seem older than they are (and teachers you do like always seem younger). She had gray hair cut in a bob. She wore glasses. Her classroom was devoid of any sort of poster, décor, color, or life displayed on the wall. I cannot tell you what she looked like from the waist down because I think I saw her get out of her chair only five times during the whole of my eighth-grade year. We have this saying in education — "Are you an 'on your feet' teacher?" This means you rarely sit down; you circulate around the classroom, you visit with your students, you look at their work while they're working, and you provide corrective feedback. These are the hallmarks of an active, engaged teacher.

Ms. Glower was not an "on your feet" teacher. She sat in the front and center of the room with her overhead projector. The students sat in rows — each with a view of the screen. She would start her class by reviewing the homework from the night before.

"Any questions about last night's homework before you turn it in?" Ms. Glower would ask.

A brave student might raise their hand. She would complete the problem on the overhead, and then ask, "Any u-thuhz?"

It wasn't "Any oth-*ERS*?" It was "Any u-thuhz?" Still to this day, I can hear her say it. If I didn't know any better, I'm quite sure it is what a PTSD flashback might feel like.

Thankfully, I had several friends and acquaintances from Mr. Wilen's seventh-grade math class who were also sentenced to advanced eighth-grade math. One of them was Jimmy Holms.

I had known Jimmy since preschool. While we weren't good friends, we were friendly to each other. Over the years, I have grown to have great respect and value for those acquaintances of mine with whom I share "historical perspective." These are the people in your life, other than your family members, who have known you since you were very young. While you may not have been close to them, they have experienced a lot of what you experienced as a child. They watched you grow, and you watched them grow. When you are with such a person, they know something about you, your upbringing, or have had a shared experience with you — these are things that perhaps even your spouse, who might know you better than anyone, does not share with you. I admired Jim because he was smart and was placed in all the advanced classes. While being somewhat quiet and reserved, he had many friends. In advanced math, Jimmy sat to my left, one row in front of mine.

My classmates and I were fortunate to grow up in the small town of Tahoe City, located right on the edge of beautiful Lake Tahoe, home to some of the best snow and ski resorts in the country. The average annual snowfall is 170 inches at lake level, while the mountain peaks and ski resorts receive far more. It wasn't at all unusual to have snow days — and some years, snow weeks.

Living in an environment with such large amounts of snow presents some interesting dualities of beauty and roughness, amusement and misery, joy and panic. Where a typical school assembly might be based on the topics of character education or Read Across America, we had presentations about snow survival with experts from Tahoe Nordic Search & Rescue. During one of our school assemblies in fourth grade, we went outside, were put in small groups, and piled into snowbanks, and Search & Rescue demonstrated how to build a snow fort. Among other items that I can't remember, we were advised to always carry chocolate when skiing. It would give us quick energy in case we got lost.

The winter of 1981–82 was unusual. Where there was ordinarily great spring skiing up until Memorial Day, the ski resorts feared they would need to close early due to lack of snow. In January, there was a huge storm with lots of snowfall. February was cold and rainy, with only seven inches of snow in total for the month. March brought sunny spring skiing conditions, creating a melt-freeze effect. But that all changed in late March. In fact, according to the Central Sierra Snow Lab, the storm that began on March 27 and finally let up on

April 8 still ranks as one of the biggest snowstorms on record for Donner Summit.

Amid this huge snowstorm, it was spring break. Barely making it to the airport in time, our family took a long-planned trip to visit a family friend working as a legislative assistant in Washington, DC. While we were visiting monuments, the Smithsonian museums, and the Capitol, the snow was falling and falling and falling on our hometown. Because our friend was working in a California congressman's office, he received daily updates of the snowfall and would pass this on to us. It was in this way that we learned of the deadly avalanche at the ski resort of Alpine Meadows — and the death of Jimmy Holms. Excited by all the fresh snow, Jim had jumped off the second story of his house into the snow below, something kids would often do after a big snowfall. I don't know what caused his death. Some thought he had broken his neck and died instantly. Others believed he sunk into the snow and suffocated.

The trip changed after that. The cherry blossoms seemed different. It was a strange feeling of wanting to go home and being afraid to go home. The plane ride would have been long anyway, but it felt very long.

The community was reeling not only from Jimmy's death but also from the tragic avalanche in which several Alpine Meadows employees and tourists had died. One employee had finally been rescued after being buried for five days.

While all of us were ready to get back to school to embrace some form of structure, there was apprehension. In those days, there weren't any sort of children's or student bereavement programs offered. There weren't any counselors or social workers available to meet within the school for support. We were left to our own devices. There seemed to be this unspoken party line that we were expected to just "get on with it."

I remember going through my class schedule in my head, making a note of which classes I had had with Jim and where he had sat in those classrooms. I had great anxiety going into eighth-grade advanced math since we had sat so close to each other. I walked in. His desk was there. Empty. I was terribly sad.

Disconnected. Off-kilter. Lost. Anxious.

And vulnerable.

During class and in the days to follow, I had rambling thoughts and so many questions. The first was "Why?" This wasn't supposed to happen to thirteen-year-olds. We were too young; this had happened too early. There was this recognition that we weren't in control. I felt scared. I wondered if I was safe.

And then I wondered: *What is it like for Ms. Glower to teach to his empty chair? What is she going to do with his math papers? Does she still need to correct them? Will she correct his?*

22

Jimmy

Such weird thoughts, but I had them. *Will she give his papers back to his parents?* And then I thought about his family. *Will they want his math papers?* I thought about his mom. *What is it like when she sets the table without him?*

The chair to my left, one row in front of mine, sat empty.

But I am still here.

Chapter 3

Grandpa Al

14 years old

Grandpa Al Neft was the second-oldest of five children born to Jewish immigrants. He had three brothers and one sister. They were interesting and eccentric. Uncle Meyer, the oldest, owned a very successful strip club on Broadway in San Francisco. Aunt Sophie was the only girl. She had big, poofy hair and was an artist. Uncle Harry died of a heart attack at sixty. Uncle Sam was the youngest. Sam played the drums and always had a smile on his face. My grandpa Al was tall and always wore a Lacoste cardigan sweater. He was quite talented in the arts and loved golf. He painted and played the saxophone.

After his retirement, Grandpa was either in his studio painting or on the course golfing. Whether by intention or coincidence, he was interested in things he could do alone. Perhaps he was just independent. I recall that Al was sometimes in trouble with my grandmother for this. He had a reputation within my family for being a bit selfish. I didn't understand why. Grandpa Al seemed so happy being with himself and being by himself. He didn't always require the company of others in the way other personalities might desire.

When I was very young, my grandparents owned a little A-frame log cabin on the south shore of Lake Tahoe, right on the golf course. It had a metal roof that reflected the sun. My parents would drop us off to stay with them for the weekend. I loved it. One time, in his yellow Lacoste cardigan sweater, my grandpa stacked up all the pillows, one on top of the other until it was quite high. He then put me on top of the pillow stack, belly-side down, with my arms out like an airplane. He sat back down on the couch below. With his hand cupped around his mouth, he shouted, "How's the weather up there?" I thought it was the funniest thing ever.

I don't think he was selfish. Grandpa Al was just true to himself.

Fast-forward to high school, which is a blur. After-school sports. Homework. Social activities. Student government. Boys. Football games. It didn't seem like I was home very much, busy being selfish and petty, no doubt. In the early spring of my freshman year, there was a lot of activity in the house very early one morning. It was a school day. My mom came in to tell me that my dad had left for the airport to fly down to Palm Springs. My grandfather had had a heart attack and passed away. I cried. It was my first experience in the death of a blood relative.

Getting ready for the funeral was stressful. When your body is growing fast, as teenagers' bodies do, you quickly outgrow clothes, including the ones needed for funerals. Our little town of Tahoe City didn't have clothing stores with dress clothes. This caused my mom a great deal of concern. Before catching the plane from Reno to Palm Springs, we went to Macy's to hastily find appropriate attire for a funeral.

My older brother went to the men's department. I went to the women's. I wasn't yet a woman, but the clothes in the girls' department no longer fit me. It was that awkward time. We found a lavender-colored pencil skirt. I now know why I didn't like that skirt — it was midi-length. Midi-length skirts don't stop at the knee to show off the calf, but they don't make it all the way down to the ankle either, which better capitalizes on the silhouette. They just stop right in the middle. Midi-length skirts represent indecision. Fish or cut bait.

In Palm Springs, my brother and I had our own hotel room with a connecting door to our parents'. It was at this time the final episode of the longest-running TV sitcom, M*A*S*H, was aired. I was disturbed by the ending in which Alan Alda's character, Hawkeye, goes crazy. Regardless of the upsetting finale, the M*A*S*H episode was a good distraction for a minute. And then it was back to that unsettling feeling in my stomach that wouldn't go away.

My family was going through something we hadn't experienced before. My grandpa was gone. My grandmother had been sideswiped by the sudden loss. My dad had lost his dad. My mom was trying to be the calm presence holding it together for everyone. And yet, I felt some sense of relief that things were happening in their natural order. I was so grateful that both my parents and brother were alive. If we were to experience a death in the family, this was the order in which it was supposed to happen. Nonetheless, everything felt surreal and unsettling, and no more *M*A*S*H*.

All that and an ill-fitting skirt.

It is interesting to me that although I can recall such details as what I wore and what the end-of-an-era TV-show distraction was, I cannot recollect anything about the service in the temple. I can't remember the prayers, who else was there, or the reception afterward. It's blank.

But I *do* remember going to the grave.

We drove in a procession following the hearse. I had seen hearses on TV but never in real life, and certainly not one used for a family member. When we arrived at the grave, my dad, uncle, and grandpa's brothers carried the casket to the graveside. It was a heavy one. Grandpa Al had been a tall man. The smell of fresh, moist dirt hung in the air. I was struck by the gaping hole in the ground and the huge mound of displaced dirt immediately off to the side. The hole was very deep, a perfect rectangle.

The rabbi said some prayers. The casket was lowered into the grave with a mechanized crank until it could go no further. Once it had been lowered, the straps were slowly withdrawn with a hand crank. I can't remember who cranked the handle. I was engrossed. It was very quiet. I heard the squeaking of the crank, and the wind, and the palms of the tree. Palm leaves rubbing together in the wind make a unique sound.

I remember thinking, *We're standing at a grave. My grandpa is gone, but what remains of him is in that casket down there at the bottom of the grave. This isn't a movie. This is happening. This is real.* The pettiness of the purple skirt — gone. Humbled. While the family and friends watched, my dad and uncle went to the pile of fresh dirt displaced from the large hole. They each took a handful and tossed it on the casket below. I did not see this coming. Now I know the Jewish tradition teaches that one of the most important divine rules or commandments that can be performed is helping a loved one find their resting place. Placing the earth in the grave is an act of love and service.

Of this whole experience, what stayed in my mind all these years is the image of my dad taking a handful of dirt and tossing it on my grandpa's casket. My dad and my uncle thus became participants, having buried their dad.

It felt complete. It was complete.

Chapter 4

Chad

21 years old

Some of my best memories of middle and high school were those of experiencing loads and loads of laughter. I just remember laughing a ton. I remember the kind of laughter when you aren't supposed to laugh and you try to hold it in, then start laughing harder still. Or the kind of laughter where it hurts and tears come to your eyes, and you have a hard time catching your breath. Then you take a deep sigh, and you can feel endorphins being released throughout your body.

Living at Lake Tahoe, we centered our recreational activities on the beautiful lake and beaches in the summer and the snow in the winter. During high school, this included skiing both after school on the ski team and on weekends. There was a cadre of us who would walk through the neighborhood every Saturday and Sunday morning to the ski shuttle stop on top of Dollar Hill across from the 7-Eleven. The shuttle ride usually took about thirty to forty-five minutes, picking up both tourists and locals along the way, including schoolmates. You never knew who might be waiting at the bus stop.

My memories of riding the ski shuttle are just as rich as my memories of skiing. There was always lots of gossiping, sharing of stories, goofing off, teasing, and laughter. Because there was only one road to Alpine Meadows, during the busy ski season and in particular during the holidays, it would sometimes take two hours each way to get to and from the ski resort. At times, we would spend more time on the bus than we would on the ski hill. We all had ski passes, so it didn't much matter how many runs we got in that day — it was a social event.

The ski shuttle was entertainment. And *if* things got dull, we would create excitement by throwing food at each other. Gorp, as we called it, now referred to as trail mix, made for the best ammunition. The nuts and raisins — they were heavy enough to throw and made a noticeable impact. Often missing our intended target, we would hit a "turkey"[2] instead, thus creating even more commotion and something to snicker about. Periodically, we got kicked off the bus for being too rowdy. Thank

---

2. The locals affectionately referred to the tourists as "turkeys." When the turkeys visited, the town changed. It became very busy; traffic was (and still is) heavy. The lines became long everywhere. The ski hill became crowded in the winter, and the beaches filled in the summers. But we needed those turkeys to feed the economy, so it was a love-hate relationship.

goodness there was a pay phone at Lucky's Grocery Store on the edge of town to call our parents for a ride.

It was from these early experiences that I learned I am drawn to certain people because when I am with them, I know something interesting and unusual will happen. These people draw experiences to themselves that I wouldn't otherwise have. Those experiences go together with either the laugh when you're trying not to laugh or that deep gut laugh accompanied by tears rolling down your cheeks. Chad was one of those people.

Chad moved to our street, Tahoma Avenue, right before our sixth-grade year. He had blue eyes, longish curly hair like a surfer's, a pointy chin, and a crooked smile. He had such capacity for laughter and was always in search of adventure. I don't remember him getting in trouble at school; however, there was a fair amount on his part of pushing hard against the boundaries.

He embodied curiosity, enthusiasm, and optimism.

He lived life with a nonstop "kid in a candy store" attitude. When Chad was around, you knew there would be fun and joy because he was that kind of person. He never took anything too seriously. There was a lightness about him. Chad was provocative and interesting, and while spending time with him, I was always wondering with a smile, *What will happen next?*

On my fourteenth birthday, I had a large group of girls over to hang out and have dinner. Chad and our mutual friend—also his next-door neighbor—Tim, crashed the party. Chad gave me a hacky sack for my birthday, and we all went outside on the driveway, stood in a circle, and began playing. It was such a metaphor for who he was, drawing people together, standing in a circle, and having fun.

And Chad loved music. It was he who first introduced me to the Grateful Dead, and when I didn't understand that Ziggy Stardust was David Bowie's fictional stage persona, it was Chad who explained. He would often ski listening to his Sony Walkman. At the end of the day, while waiting for the shuttle, we'd talk about which songs he listened to on which ski runs and which ones best fit the ride among the moguls.

We were both off doing our things in high school, and then I moved out of town for college. We didn't stay in touch, but we'd run into each other when I returned to the lake for summers. I worked as a waitress serving breakfast and sometimes scooping ice cream in the afternoon. He worked down the street on the dock renting jet skis. Always humming the Grateful Dead, he'd drop in for a scoop of ice cream and we'd have a quick catch-up.

Spring of 1990 I had graduated and was working in Santa Monica. I received a call from a friend who told me the news that Chad had died in an accident while extreme skiing.

Chad

The air was knocked out of me.

I thought about Chad. I tried to remember the last time we had seen each other. I was searching for a connection. What did we talk about?

In the days that followed, I thought about what Chad would have experienced in the seconds before he died. I thought about where he was skiing. How had he gotten there? What had caused the accident? Had he been afraid? There was some peace in knowing that Chad had been doing exactly what he loved doing, pursuing joy, seeking adventure, pushing the boundaries — no doubt with curiosity, enthusiasm, and optimism.

And I like to think that he would have thought, *I wonder what will happen next.*

When Chad died, I was in my early twenties. My brain had developed and matured past the point of being "the immortal teenager."

It was Chad's death that made me start to face the hard truth of my own mortality.

Chapter 5

Maple Ridge Lane

In the mid-'90s, a year after my husband, Tim, passed the bar exam and started working for a large firm in the big city, we decided we would move back to Tim's hometown of Bend, Oregon. It was here he would hang out his own shingle. We sold our little starter home in the valley and began looking for a home to buy in Bend. We thought this would happen quickly. In October, we moved into Tim's mom's ranch, also his childhood home, with the hopes of being there only three months at most. But bless my mother-in-law's heart for being patient, it turned into eleven months. We finally found a home in May of the following year. It was a three-bedroom craftsman house built in 1920, several blocks from the river. The house was darling but in terrible disrepair. While still living at Pat's house, we began our first of many gut-and-remodels.

Living on Pat's property was different. I hadn't experienced large acreage and privacy like this before; the ranch was about twenty-six acres. Pat (my mother-in-law) had three or four horses and six cows. Since Central Oregon is high desert, irrigation is required to water the pastures. Tim's dad had passed away eight years earlier, so Tim was the natural live-in ranch hand to help fix fences, feed the animals, change the irrigation pipes, and run the tractor.

I began substitute teaching, and at the end of the school year, I secured a full-time job teaching kindergarten, to begin the following fall. I took a job for the summer working the counter at the new-to-Bend artisan bakery.

It was the second weekend of July. There was a lot going on that weekend: the annual horse races in Prineville and the Bend Summer Festival. The bakery attained a booth for the festival. On Saturday, I worked the shop, while the other employees worked the festival. I was scheduled to work the booth on Sunday.

It was midafternoon Saturday. I was done with my shift and returned home to Pat's house. Pat was just leaving with a friend to go to the races. Typically, we would have gone to the races too, but we had opted not to go this year. Tim was in and out of the house working on ranch projects. He drove his truck down to the lower pasture to fire up the battery on the old Ford tractor.

I changed out of my bakery clothes and was in the kitchen. The doorbell rang. This was unusual. The doorbell rarely rings when you live away from town. In fact, it's sort of unusual for cars to drive in on the property at all. And typically, if we were out on the property, as Tim was, and saw the car, we would greet the visitors before they reached the door.

I opened the door. There was a family of four there: a mom and dad and two high school–aged teenagers — brother and sister. I later learned they were the Jones family.

"Call 9-1-1! Call 9-1-1! Call 9-1-1!" Mrs. Jones was frantic, crying. "He has a gun to her head! He has a gun to her head!"

I motioned to all of them to quickly come in and asked her to follow me to the kitchen where the phone was plugged into the wall. I called 9-1-1 but soon realized I was ill-equipped to give any details to the emergency dispatcher other than our physical address. I handed the phone to Mrs. Jones.

Meanwhile, I turned to the dad and kids to find out more details.

Mr. Jones told me that their daughter, Laney, and the daughter of another family, the Middletons, were good friends. They had had a sleepover the night before at the Middletons' house. Laney had forgotten to bring her shoes home. The Joneses had been heading out of town for the weekend, and Laney had asked if they could swing by the Middletons' on their way, to grab her shoes. When they approached the entryway of the house, they saw the divorced Mrs. Middleton with her estranged boyfriend's arms locked around her head and neck, with a gun to her head. The Jones family quickly left to seek help. Pat's house was the closest option.

The Middleton daughter soon joined us. Her mom had told her to leave and find safety.

My thoughts went to her. And then I thought of my Tim. Was he OK? He was on the east side of the neighbor's house, not far from where this was all taking place. Was he in the barn? Was he in the pasture? Did he know what was going on? If he did, he would have intervened because he is that kind of person.

I asked Mr. Jones if he had seen my husband or knew of his whereabouts. He hadn't and didn't. Clearly, then, Tim didn't know what was going on. But what if he found out? Or maybe he had tried to intervene before their arrival and been shot? I was in a quiet panic. Worried about him. Worried about the neighbor. Worried about the daughter who had seen her mom being held hostage at gunpoint.

Mrs. Jones hung up and said the police were on their way. We moved to the living room, gathering ourselves.

Time was beginning to do weird things. It felt as though it was bending. Slowing. As though everything was in slow motion. I couldn't tell how much time had passed. How long had the family been in the house with me? Had it been just a few minutes, ten minutes? How long had she been on the phone with the dispatcher? *Shouldn't the police be here by now?*

Meanwhile, the six of us felt like we should do something, so we went out into the driveway to see if we could learn more or see anything, but also trying to be safe and far enough away. The daughter of the hostage was crying and screaming. We offered comfort, but how do you do that for someone when a gun is being held to their loved one's head? There is no comfort. Safety is the only comfort we could provide for her mom, and we were unable to do that until the police arrived. What should we do to help the mom to safety without putting ourselves at risk?

And where is Tim? Is he OK?

From the driveway, we heard a vehicle starting up in front of the Middletons' house, which we could see in the distance. The gunman put the hostage in her SUV on the passenger's side. He got in the driver's side and started the car. We thought we heard gunshots but couldn't quite tell. The SUV had a mattress strapped to the top of it. He began driving toward the entrance. The unsecured part of the mattress flipped up in the wind, much like a visor on a baseball cap.

As they drove by, the victim was leaning against the door. Her body was slumped abnormally. As he passed us slowly, the gunman pointed his gun at each of us. He moved his gun to point it at each one of us as though to readjust his target. It still felt like it was all in slow motion.

Was this really happening? Had this man just driven by, pointing a gun at us point-blank? Did this just happen? I snapped out of it and thought, *We are idiots. Why are we out here putting ourselves in the way of danger? What are we thinking?*

My legs were shaking. My hands were sweating. The adrenaline surged. I could feel my heart pulse through my body. I felt it beating. I heard it beating.

I thought about the mom, about her leaning against the passenger door. We were trying to help — as if just our presence could help.

The daughter wailed. None of us said anything.

As soon as the vehicle passed us, I immediately ran to get to the pasture. I didn't want to go near the driveway in case he came back. Why weren't the cops here yet? I thought about time again. I couldn't get a bearing on it.

I leaped the fence and began running through the pasture as fast as my legs could carry me. In my mind's eye, my legs were moving in slow motion. Time kept bending. I avoided the horses, but they knew. Horses know fear. The tall grass made running hard and scratched my legs. My lungs were burning. I couldn't remember the last time I had run this hard — middle school? I finally reached the fence, climbed over, and ran across the dirt road to the lower pasture.

I saw Tim riding the old Ford tractor. There he was. He was riding south, unaware and safe from recent events. I said a prayer of thanks. He was going back and forth with his back to me. Knowing he would turn in my direction soon, I began waving and motioning as dramatically as I could, occasionally bending over with my hands on my knees to catch my breath. He saw. Now time began to behave normally again; he arrived sooner than I expected. Through broken breaths, I told him what was happening.

When we arrived back at the house, everyone was still outside. We saw the police car had intercepted the SUV at the fork in the road next to the big juniper tree. Two or three policemen were each on one knee with both hands on their gun, all of them aiming at the driver — still in the car. I wondered, living in such a small town, if this was the first time these cops had seen this type of violence. From the inside, a puff of dark smoke filled the car.

The driver had shot himself.

The police opened the driver's door and pulled him out. He was dead. They laid him in the driveway. They got to the hostage on the passenger side; she had been shot — six times — but she was still alive. A policeman came to the house. We were still in the driveway. He told Tim that Life Flight was on the way, and he needed Tim to get the cows off to one side of the pasture so that the helicopter could land in the middle pasture. Her daughter heard the name Life Flight, and the only word I can use to describe her reaction is *anguish*. Fall-to-your-knees anguish.

Disbelief. Crying. Wailing.

Tim hopped the fence and began waving his arms in an effort to drive the cows. "Come, cows. Move, cows," he encouraged. They were most unhappy about this disruption but acquiesced. We could hear the beat of the helicopter blades, and the tall grass started to whip sideways. Crying. Sobbing. Having to lift their knees high to work through the tall grass, the first responders used a stretcher and loaded her in. Tim returned to the house. The helicopter lifted off.

"No," screamed the daughter. "No!"

I don't remember doing what I did next — my husband reminded me — but while this was happening, I went over to the daughter and put my arm around her and held her. The helicopter got quieter in the distance. His dead body was still on the driveway.

Again I wondered, *How much time has passed?*

The police came into the house and began interviewing each of us separately to get an idea of what had transpired. I told the policeman everything as I remembered it unfolding but was unable to identify time frames.

Cell phones were relatively new, but they were able to track down Mr. Middleton, who was in Eugene. He was on his way. This gave me a greater sense of relief, knowing the daughter would now be with her dad.

By the time Pat returned from the horse races later that evening, it was just Tim and me alone in the house. The dead body was off the driveway, the cops were gone, and the cows were back to grazing in their pasture that had been used as a helicopter landing pad. It felt quiet and eerie. Bizarre. I felt dazed, like I was floating. I couldn't hold a thought. I didn't want to think about it, but I didn't know what to think about.

As we told Pat the story, she sat in shock.

The mom did not make it through the night. My heart ached for the daughter who not only had lost her mom but would have this memory to carry for a lifetime. How do you unsee that? How do you unfeel that?

The next day, I went to work at the bakery booth at the Bend Summer Festival. I told my colleagues the story. They responded in disbelief. They were surprised I had come to work that day. While I didn't want to leave them shorthanded, in truth, mostly, I needed to be out and engaged in the world. My coworkers understood — I was there, but not there. Not apathetic, but in a different place. I was detached.

Is that what shock feels like?

This was trauma.

We had witnessed a murder-suicide right there on the edge of the front pasture.

In the days that followed, we recounted the events and also learned more about what had happened. Earlier that Saturday, the estranged boyfriend had been driving up and down the dirt driveway to the house. Apparently, he was checking to see if she was there. This was churning up the dust, which is a scourge for those living on a dirt road. At one point, Tim motioned to him to please slow down, and he waved back, agitated while slowing down. Later in the day, the estranged boyfriend parked at a nearby dead-end road and walked through some pastures before sneaking into the Middleton house. He hid while waiting for her to arrive; then he ambushed her.

I have often thought about the way chance, randomness, and the timing of events looped and threaded into each other that day — for the Jones family to come by at the time they did to retrieve the shoes, and how that perhaps saved the daughter's life. This was obviously not something the perpetrator could have anticipated. Without the Joneses intercepting and coming up to the house, would the police ever have been called? I thought about how Tim had been in the lower pasture on the tractor. Would things have unfolded differently if he had been up at the house? There was the fact that Tim and I were even still living there at the time and that we had decided not to go to the races that year. How differently would things have turned out had the assailant pulled the trigger as he was driving by us all standing there in the driveway? And then how Pat missed the whole thing when she would usually have been home.

Chance. Randomness. Timing.

Fate?

I've also considered that living on such a quiet, protected, bucolic piece of property hadn't protected the neighbor, or any of us, from violence. While crime and violence are most often associated with densely populated communities, here it had happened right in the front pasture. I've lived in cities. I visit cities frequently and have never had a gun pointed at me point-blank. And here out in the quiet, remote countryside...it could easily have become a drive-by shooting. And since then, as life continues to unfold, we've seen this happen in the most unexpected places, such as elementary schools and churches, synagogues, theaters, concert venues and grocery stores.

Chance, randomness, and the timing of events looped and threaded into each other.

Into each other.

We are all connected.

Chapter 6

Arlene

31 years old

A year after my parents divorced, my dad began dating Arlene. She was tiny and feisty with glistening blond hair like Doris Day's. A consummate realtor, she took her profession seriously and was successful. She had been married and divorced once before and had never had children. She was a member of the Soroptimists and believed in women supporting women.

Arlene wore wide-wale cords with a turtleneck and her nails were always manicured, long and painted frosty pink. She was German and loved reading biographies. Frank was her maiden name. I once read in a sports car magazine that it's not unusual for Germans to take greater pride in the car they drive than in the dwelling they live in. While perhaps a stereotype, that was Arlene — she put little thought or effort into the décor of her house but always drove a sports car. (She drove an Audi with a stick and, before that, a BMW.) Arlene knew who she was and possessed a quiet confidence.

I was sixteen when my dad began seeing Arlene. It wasn't easy for me, but Arlene made it as easy as anyone could ever have made it for a child of divorce. She understood that there was real estate in my father's heart that could never be bought, sold, or traded for anyone but his children. That "deed" remained for us in perpetuity. This is a rare insight for anyone in a blended family, particularly for someone who never had children herself. Even at the naive age of sixteen, I understood this characteristic in her was unique. We held a mutual, unspoken respect for each other.

My dad was so joyful and happy with her. It was hard to hold any sort of angst or weirdness when he was clearly flourishing. Arlene had an insatiable travel bug. She traveled all around the world, sometimes with my dad but mostly without. I loved the fact that they could be supportive yet independent of each other's hobbies even if they didn't always share them. What a beautiful model of how it should be. It is easier to appreciate it at the age of fifty-six, but I somehow understood even then that this was healthy. Arlene and my dad discussed marrying, but they never did. They had such a wonderful thing going that Arlene didn't want to do anything that would compromise or ruin what they had.

Arlene taught me how to knit. She was amazing. She could knit anything. Argyles or intarsia, she could read or bring to life intricate patterns. Her brain was always sharp, and I think working through complicated knitting patterns was an expression of this. Arlene would work on only one knitting project at a time. She would finish it and *then* move on to the next. This amazed me and still does since I am more of the ADHD type who might have three or four different knitting projects going on at once. It was and still is admirable. There is something to be said for the satisfaction of completion.

Arlene watched me finish high school and graduate from college, cheered me during my bike trip I took across the country, and then took the same bike to cycle across France. With my dad, she was there when I got married. She was a witness to fourteen very important transitional years in my life.

Before meeting my dad, Arlene had breast cancer. She had had a mastectomy, and her cancer was in re-mission. She had had both breast reconstruction and a facelift. I just loved the fact that she didn't really care about what others thought. Her mantra was "Live fast, die young, and look good in a box."

One early December, after my husband and I had been married for several years, my dad announced that he and Arlene were coming to Bend at Christmas for a week. This surprised me since they lived in Palm Desert, and Bend is quite cold in December. They came. It was ten below when they arrived.

Ten below.

We watched a lot of movies together. We ate a lot, and I remember a little cabin fever. During the middle of their stay, Arlene had a terrible nosebleed that wouldn't stop, so much so, that we took her to the emergency room. On the way to the ER, my dad told us that Arlene's cancer had returned, but they hadn't wanted to tell us and sour the holiday. The doctors cauterized the blood vessel in her nose. I didn't understand the severity of what my dad had said. Three months later, we visited them for spring break. Arlene was on oxygen. And still it didn't sink in.

Arlene had put out a bowl of M&Ms to nibble on. My husband said to me, "Look, honey, they have desert-themed M&Ms." They were pastel-colored, which was a trendy color in the late '90s, the desert scheme.

"No, honey," I said back to him. "Those are Easter-colored M&Ms."

Again, why do I remember strange, insignificant, stupid facts like the color of the candy when big, looming, elephant-in-the-room cues, *such as oxygen machines*, didn't seem to hold my attention in the same way? This is something I now know you have to pay attention to. In hindsight, it can only be called denial.

We returned to Bend in late March. Three weeks later, my dad called, saying that Arlene was in the hospital. She was having trouble breathing. I asked if I should come down.

"No," my dad said. At the time, both my dad and Arlene thought the hospital was a temporary stop, having no idea how very sick she was.

We spoke almost every day. She was there for maybe a week. The cancer had spread to her lungs. There was so much scar tissue on her lungs that they could no longer tell in the X-rays if they were looking at scar tissue or at cancer.

She died. My dad called me. In the thirty years I had known him, I had never known him to be fragile. Now he was. Arlene had requested, both verbally and in her will, that there be no funeral or service. My dad was planning to move ahead with her wishes until one of Arlene's best friends stepped in. She told my dad that it was not fair to deny the people who loved her the opportunity to honor her and say goodbye. My dad agreed and, going against Arlene's wishes, went ahead to plan a service. He asked for my help.

At the time, I was teaching kindergarten. I had four days of bereavement granted, and I took that in addition to two weekend days. I flew down there on a Tuesday. On Wednesday, we went to the funeral chapel to finalize the service and to the florist to pick out the flowers. Some friends in their community had planned and hosted the meal afterward. My brother came down. It was a beautiful ceremony.

For the days remaining, my dad, brother, and I spent

most of our time together sitting on my dad's back patio. I was not ready to leave. I was just not ready, full stop. My dad wasn't ready. I don't think my brother was ready either. If I had it to do over again, I would have stayed another week. The kindergarteners would have been fine. The reduced paycheck would have been fine. It just didn't matter. Being with my dad was what should have mattered.

I lament the fact that Arlene never met our children. She never had children of her own, and I know she would have absolutely delighted to watch them grow and change and call her Grandma — she'd have been enchanted by the whole new experience.

Several years later, Arlene visited me in a dream. She was standing in front of the fireplace in her house by the lake. She was wearing a turtleneck and her wide-wale cords, and her hands were beautifully manicured, just as they always had been. I noticed her long, tan fingers with smooth, buttery skin. She reached out to me, touched my hand, and smiled. Enchanted.

It was for real right there.

When I woke, I knew something special had just happened, and it felt as though it would all be OK.

Chapter 7

James

43 years old

August might be one of my least favorite months. In the high desert of Central Oregon, the days grow shorter while the nights grow cooler. A thunderstorm might visit, sparking both lightning and forest fires. There is a palpable feeling in the air that change is coming. As my life as a student and then a teacher has revolved around the academic calendar, August is also synonymous with the return to school. Sometimes this can mean a feeling of excitement. Sometimes this can mean a feeling of dread. It is usually a combination. In either case, August has an arousing effect that creates uncertainty. It is equal parts anticipation and waning.

It was the third Saturday of August; midmorning; pancakes; bacon; sticky countertops. Inside, I was cleaning up breakfast while getting everyone packed to make a summer's-end visit to the lake. In the last weekends of summer, our family shoehorns in as many summer activities as possible before it is time to buy school supplies.

Sunscreen. Beach towels. Watermelon. Outside, my husband was washing the car, something he loves to do. The Rolling Stones were playing.

The house phone rang. I looked at the caller ID and noticed it was from Idaho, which meant it was my brother-in-law, Grant. While they were eighteen years apart in age, my husband and he had always been close. They spoke frequently, often three to four times a week, so it was not unusual for him to call at any hour. I answered it.

It was Grant's wife. I heard her sobbing and crying and speaking to me, but I was unable to understand what she was saying. I immediately thought something had happened to Grant, as he had suffered a life-threatening accident eleven months earlier and had been in and out of surgeries ever since. I told her that I was going to get Tim.

He heard more than his name when I called out — my tone was fueled with fear and panic. At this moment in time, Tim and I had been together for a total of twenty-one years and married for eighteen of them. When you have been with someone that long, you know when it is urgent just by the way they call your name. He dropped the hose and rushed inside.

"It's Jean. Something has happened. I cannot understand her," I said as I handed him the phone. I stood nearby and listened while he worked through the conversation. He asked a few questions. He listened. He heard.

He understood.

His expression changed. He said goodbye and hung up as the tears welled up.

"James died," he said in almost a whisper as he cried.

James was Grant's son. He had been twenty-eight years old.

I hugged Tim. It was not the time to ask questions, and he didn't have answers even if I had done so. Those would come in the days to follow. Sobbing, he went back outside and picked up the hose, in shock and disbelief. Sometimes rote activities are most useful at these times. Our hands are busy while our minds are trying to make sense of things even if there is no making sense of the situation.

I watched him wash the car. He was scrubbing the wheels now. I watched, and he kept repeating as if saying it aloud would somehow help it sink in better, "I can't believe he's gone. I can't believe he's gone," over and over between sobs.

We didn't go to the lake that day.

Two weeks later, our family went to Spokane, the closest major town, to be with the family and attend the funeral. The night before the funeral, the family and close friends all gathered at the home of James's mom, Cindy. There was a lot of food delivered by family friends. Casseroles, appetizers, desserts, vegetable trays, dips, and chips. It was a bountiful spread of compassion.

It was the same gathering of relatives and friends we had last seen at James's sister's rehearsal dinner (and wedding) five years earlier, although there were a few new faces. At the rehearsal dinner, we had been celebrating. Now we were grieving. And it was a different kind of grief, excruciating grief where there are no answers. While we were all glad to see each other, we were suffering from the event that had brought us together. I can only describe the conversation as random. We would look at pictures, share memories, laugh, and then cry. Then the conversation would change to something about pop culture or a "Hey, did you hear about..." moment. It was as though these were desperate attempts to feel normal, despite the knowledge that there wasn't going to be normal again for a long time, if ever.

The funeral was the next morning. Only a small group of family and close friends were invited to the graveside service, which took place before the funeral service and the reception immediately after. We drove to the cemetery. This was the first time our children had been to a cemetery or a burial service or funeral. I recall that on the drive to the cemetery, Tim and I told them what to expect.

We parked near the office. It was quite a walk to the burial site, mostly uphill. There was a canopy over a carpet with white chairs unfolded and placed in three or four neat rows. The flaps of the canopy were blowing in the wind. Off to the side was James in the casket. The casket was most unusual. It wasn't rectangular and polished with shiny wood and brass fittings. Rather, it was off-white and smooth. It had a rounded top with silver snaps at the seams. It had two drawers at the bottom to store special mementos to be buried with him. And it was made of plastic or laminate casing. This was so appropriate to James and his personality. He had not been rectangular or formal at all. He had been easygoing, calm, and anything but stuffy.

The family sat under the canopy; close friends created a half circle standing on the grass. The priest was in front. The casket was off to the right. There was no hole in the ground to be seen. There were no cranks nearby to lower it in the ground. After the short service, with a marker in the color of our choice, we were invited to write a message on the coffin. Now I understood the unique casket. We each took a moment to write our message to James. It was a beautiful way to say goodbye, so personal.

Next was the funeral service, of which I have no memory.

After the funeral, we all walked over to the nearby community center, which I think was also the church school's gymnasium. My daughter's hand was in mine. As we entered the building, my eyes were drawn upward. I saw the small, stark, industrial rectangular windows with light clawing to get inside. The spongey holes in the cinder blocks were locked in time covered with thick, gray, shiny latex paint. The grooves where the cinder blocks joined each other were deep and inviting. It looked as though it would be satisfying to run my finger down the gully between the blocks, but instead, I kept hold of my daughter's hand. What made me want to touch the wall — something I would have done during PE class in elementary school — especially at a time like this?

I scanned the room. It was filled with round tables surrounded by chairs. There were rectangular tables filled with food off to the left. A large screen was in place at the far end of the room. People were talking in low voices, generating a collective murmur. More people were behind us, still walking in.

My eyes were drawn upward to the windows again.

Then I noticed it.

It was a sensation I had never felt before. The feeling wasn't coming from within me, but rather it was happening around me. It was happening to me, like when you walk outside in the hot July sunshine after being in a dark, air-conditioned theater all afternoon.

Helplessness. Heartbrokenness. Pain. Pure and total sadness. Anguish. Yet also — humility. Forgiveness. Void of judgment. Compassion. Sincerity and innocence in the confusion of it all. It was depleted of ego, falseness, vanity, pride, or pretension.

Raw.

Authentic.

Is this what mercy feels like?

Is this what grace feels like?

James, are you here? Is this you?

Is this the divine? And if it is, how is it that such a painful loss could reveal the divine?

In the absence of distraction or preoccupation, this was an uncommon occurrence of a rare level of awareness — that everyone in the room was completely present and there for no other reason than to honor James.

If I had left the room and all the people in the room, the sensation would have stopped. It was a collective sum of the people and emotions felt in the room. It lingered while we ate, watched the video montage of James's life, sat at the round tables, talked to each other, and told stories of James.

And in this complete and total authenticity — it was comforting and warm and beautiful.

James, are you here? Is this you?
We have lost you, James. Yet you are everywhere.

●

James was a victim of the opioid epidemic. He accidentally and tragically overdosed.

Chapter 8

Wally

44 years old

Annie was seven, just getting ready to start second grade. It was Labor Day weekend. Tim returned from an hour's drive with five tons of hay to store for the winter. He began stacking the hay in the barn. A while later, he came to the house.

He called for Annie.

"Honey, can you find me a large box and line it with a towel and blankets? I have a surprise for you."

"What is it, Daddy? What is it?" she asked.

Oh no, I thought. *This can only mean one thing.*

While unloading the bales, he had found five kittens, maybe three weeks old. Apparently, when the hay was loaded, a hay squeeze was used, which bundles multiple bales together and loads them on the trailer. It saves hours of time and energy. This happy little litter was safely nestled within. Annie was beside herself with excitement.

"What about the momma cat?" I asked. "Shouldn't we take them back?" It was clearly a question from a farm girl who hadn't grown up on a farm.

"She's a barn cat. She'll be fine. She's already moved on," remarked Tim.

She's going to get mastitis, I thought.

I called the vet, a friend of ours. He graciously took my call on the holiday weekend. He instructed me to head to the pet store or the local emergency pet clinic to find some powdered kitten formula to bottle-feed them. All five of them would need to be bottle-fed two to three times a day until they were able to eat wet food. At first, I was overwhelmed by the idea. How would I make this happen? But a teeny-tiny kitten has a tiny stomach, so it didn't take long to fill it. The formula was administered with a little syringe. I quickly learned to wear jeans when I was doing this as the kittens would climb up my legs to get fed.

You feel quite loved when five kittens are crawling all over you — even if it is for food. I grew to rather enjoy this time of day, and for the next month, my daily schedule revolved around feeding the kittens. Even when they weren't eating, we'd go in the laundry room and sit on the floor to have kitten time. It was joyous and fun. All the worries of the day faded away during kitten time.

The runt of the litter quickly became my favorite. He was tiny and aggressive. If I was standing up at the washing machine, feeding one of the other kittens, he would claw into my pants and crawl up my leg. He ate quickly and plentifully, making his little tummy sag. When he walked, he waddled. So, we named him Wally. I would carry him up on my shoulder near the nape of my neck and that became his spot.

The time came when the kittens were getting big and wanting to explore. Our son asked if we could keep all five kittens. "No, but we can keep Wally," I promptly answered. When the litter turned old enough, eight weeks, we immediately had them neutered or spayed. Two of the kittens went to a friend, two went to a no-kill cat shelter where they quickly found homes, and Wally stayed.

Wally was a great cat. Very cuddly. For the next two years, I was frequently writing. I would sit on the couch with my laptop, and he would sit next to me, sometimes crawling up to my neck like he used to do when he was a kitten. Every night at eight o'clock after I turned the house down for sleep, we'd head to the bedroom where we'd play hide-and-seek before he was tucked into his laundry room at night.

When Wally turned two, he brought home a stray cat who had hidden in the cabinet of our barbeque. I was away on a business trip when he showed up.

Annie called, all excited. "Mom! Wally brought home a kitten. Can we keep him?"

"No" was my first response. I was thinking, *Oh my gosh, they keep finding us! These cats. What is it with them?*

I now realize that when you're a cat person, they find you.

It turned out that this poor kitten was terribly afraid. Finally, after enough food and cream, he had the courage to come into the house. Every time he visited us, he would immediately race into Annie's bedroom where he would hide in the box spring of her bed. I named him Fraidy, as in fraidy-cat.

Not too long after Fraidy came into our lives, Wally seemed less playful. I thought it was because Fraidy had changed the dynamic in the house but soon realized he didn't feel well. The vet informed us Wally's kidneys were failing. He was dying.

Heartbroken, I gathered the family, and we all went down to the vet where we were able to hold him and pet him and tell him that we loved him. It was our children's first experience of loss and an opportunity to have the experience of being able to say goodbye to their pet.

We all cried. We all held him. We all said goodbye. And we were lucky to live on a large property where we could make a little grave for him.

Tim made a little wooden sign, and Annie painted it with his name, hearts, and flowers.

Wally

And when seeing this precious little hand-painted wooden sign, I would think about Wally — and feel so glad he had been in our lives.

Chapter 9

Grant

47 years old

As I mentioned in James's chapter, Tim's brother Grant was eighteen years older than him; he was from their dad's first marriage. Despite their age difference, they were the best of friends. They enjoyed fishing, camping, hunting, riding horses, and working on projects together, such as building barns and fixing fences. He was the only one who still called Tim Timmy. Grant and Tim would talk several times a week, usually between 10:00 and 10:30 at night, typically while Grant was going through the drive-through or driving home from Walmart. They would talk about any number of things: where to apply for hunting tags, the used truck Grant was looking to buy, or the price of hay. If I could say one thing about Grant, it was that he lived fully. He was always going somewhere.

He was a middle school gym teacher in Priest River, Idaho, near the border with Washington; the kids loved him because he was just so much fun and full of surprises.

Grant would often visit us and stay for weeks at a time in the summer and over the holidays. Grant had a most interesting relationship with time. He wouldn't abide by it and was late for everything. He would drive all night to get where he was going and then, upon his arrival, sleep all day, waking up just in time for dinner. It never occurred to him that it was a zero-sum game, driving all night. Had he slept at night and then driven all day, arriving just in time for dinner — it would have ended with the same result, and he might have been more rested by following nature's well-planned circadian rhythm. Tim always said he would have been the perfect candidate for a biosphere experiment. When Grant visited, staying up until 2:00 a.m. watching the History Channel was a frequent occurrence at our house. And what was even more interesting was that we would all begin staying up late with him. We called it the Grant Effect.

One of my favorite stories about him was from when I was seven and a half months pregnant with our son. Grant had been staying with us for several days already. Driving our own cars, we all met in town for dinner. After dinner, Grant told Tim he was going to quickly swing by the store to grab a few things. He showed up two hours later, at 11:30. At this point, I was in bed already, reading Harry Potter. Tim came to get me.

"You have to come see this," he said.

We headed to the kitchen. Grant apparently thought

that, as I was pregnant, I needed more food in the house (or that was the excuse, anyway). Fresh out of the grocery sacks sitting on the counter there were: a dozen day-old donuts; a sack of bulk Brach's candy; twenty-four cans of off-brand soda, mostly lemon-lime, and a six-pack of Mountain Dew (Grant's go-to favorite); a bucket of Red Vines licorice; two boxes of cereal, Fruity Pebbles and Lucky Charms; a gallon of whole milk; and, in the freezer, two gallons of off-brand ice cream. My kitchen didn't know what to think — it had never seen so many bright colors before.

"Wow" was all I could say.

Another favorite story: It was our son's first birthday weekend. Grant arrived sometime in the middle of the night. We woke the next morning to find these enormous balloons — five of them, all different colors, tied to the barstools in the kitchen. The baby was beside himself with delight at these huge, colorful balloons. Grant had apparently dipped into a car lot after-hours and snipped the balloons off the cars.

You just had to appreciate his ability to bend the rules whenever given the chance.

Since the price of hay was often less expensive in Idaho, if he was coming down for a visit anyway, Grant would bring down several tons. This usually happened once a summer, occasionally twice. But in the summer of 2015, Grant brought us four trailer loads full.

I asked my husband, "Why does he keep bringing us hay?"

"I don't really know," replied Tim, "but we'll use it all eventually."

We always reimbursed him and paid for the fuel. But it was odd. On his last trip in early August, he came up to the house to say goodbye. Tim had left for work, the kids were off at camps, and I was the only one in the house. When he walked through the sliding glass door, I got this weird feeling. I shrugged it off and gave him a big hug goodbye.

Three weeks later, on August 31, we got the call. It was early evening. Back at his home, Grant had been unloading hay and then come into the house. He hadn't been feeling good. His wife, Jean, had encouraged him to sit down, thinking maybe he needed some food. It was almost time for dinner. Not long after, they were on their way to the ER. In the car, Grant suffered a cardiac arrest. Jean called 9-1-1, but they were quite a distance from the nearest services. She began chest compressions. Finally, after what likely felt like a lifetime, the paramedics arrived and took over. Jean then called Grant's daughter, Missy, to tell her what was happening. Missy called Tim, and all of us started praying. While Tim was on the phone with Missy, they were able to get Grant's heart beating again.

They rushed Grant to the hospital and immediately performed surgery, during which they cleared a 90 percent blockage in his left anterior descending artery (the largest coronary artery). Soon after that, they put him in a coma for twenty-four hours. The purpose of an induced coma is to reduce any anticipated brain injury that may have been caused by lack of oxygen during the cardiac arrest.

Five years prior to this, Grant had suffered a life-threatening accident—he was thrown by a mule in the middle of the outback in northern Idaho. Tim had been with him, and by a wing and many prayers, he had been airlifted out. After ten days in the ICU, he had pulled through. There had been several surgeries since, but he had always recovered.

This was what we knew. We were used to Grant recovering. It was to be expected.

But twenty-four hours after the incident, when they warmed his body and tried to bring him from the induced coma, he did not wake.

Missy called me. "The nurses told us we need to be prepared."

"What are you talking about? What are you saying—prepared for what?" I was incredulous.

"He might not wake up," she said.

Despite the CPR, despite Jean's and the first responders' efforts, due to fact that the blockage had been in the most prominent artery in his heart, Grant's heart having stopped for an extended period had kept much-needed oxygen from his brain for too long.

The nurses knew he was not going to wake up.

We weren't ready to hear this. We didn't want to hear this. We didn't believe them. How did they know, anyhow?

And then, after many phone calls, debates, and conversations, it began to sink in. I didn't know it at the time, but our grief journeys had begun. The whole unit mobilized in the same way an army moves in for battle. Everyone flew in and drove to Spokane. The whole family came. Grant's family came. Jean's family came. There were eighteen of us at one point. He was in the cardiac care unit, which only two people at a time were allowed to enter.

We bent the rules.

Since Grant had MRSA, we were required to wear smocks when visiting. I remember one evening when all eighteen of us surrounded Grant in his hospital bed in oversized yellow coverall smocks. In our tops, bottoms, and bouffant protector caps, we stood in a circle, hand in hand, praying. It was so beautiful. If only we could all be so lucky to have our beds surrounded by family, praying together as we fight to heal.

It was here that it occurred to me that he would have been ready to go, but for us. His heart had started again for us. We needed this. He had brought us together, and he had bought us time to process.

Grant was doing this for us.

He was on a ventilator, which kept his body breathing in the event it wouldn't do it on its own. It appeared to be uncomfortable for him and was very uncomfortable to watch.

We weren't ready to accept it. The next day we asked to meet with the first of two neurosurgeons to debrief us and answer our questions.

"How come when you have a stroke, your brain compensates? Why wouldn't that work now?"

"What would his life be like if he was awake?"

"How do we know he isn't just in a coma?"

"Is there any way to be sure?"

The surgeon said, "No, there isn't a way to absolutely know, but there is a way to see the activity in his brain. A brain scan."

"Can we request a brain scan, please?"

The following day, they did the brain scan.

We waited. Grant's condition didn't change. We occasionally saw him stretching his legs, or sometimes he seemed to be squeezing our hands. We were told by the medical staff this was his autonomic nervous system regulating involuntarily. We looked constantly for his eyes opening.

"Are you there, Grant? Can you hear us, Grant? Do you know we are here, Grant?"

His condition didn't change.

The next morning, while we awaited the results, I went down to the lobby of the hospital to call one of my best buddies, my spiritual soul sister. She was aware of what was happening, but I needed to check in with her.

I paced around the lobby while bringing her up-to-date, talking and crying. Her response was supportive but demanding.

"Your job right now is to be a bright, shiny light," she stated very directly.

I let that sink in. She wasn't telling me what to do. She was telling me *who* I needed to *be*.

"OK," I said. It was not just a regular *OK*; it sounded more like the way Forrest Gump would reply. It was the kind of *OK* you say when total surrender with no assurance of the outcome is required.

"My job right now is to be a bright, shiny light. I will *be* this. I don't know what this means, but I am going to try, and I will be brave."

After I hung up, we all met in the large conference room on the same floor as the cardiac unit. All of us, Grant's kids, his wife, and other family members, sat around the table. The second neurosurgeon sat off to the side with the computer in front of her. She showed us the MRI scan of Grant's brain and explained to us, from top to bottom, what he would experience if he were, in her words, "to miraculously wake."

"If he was to wake, he would no longer have his eyesight," she gently said.

She continued the cursor down the scan, moving from the top of Grant's brain to the bottom of his brain.

"If he was to wake, he would be bed-bound. And he would need to be tube-fed."

I can't remember if someone asked or if it was inherently understood that he would not be able to speak if he did wake.

My heart went out to the doctor. She had a hard job delivering such difficult news. For her, or for that matter any doctor who must deliver this type of information, there is no way to make it easier or better. The facts must be stated — honestly and candidly, with no sugar coating, so that the family can decide.

The operative word was *if* — if he were to miraculously wake, was this how he would want to live?

Since he had had so many surgeries recently, there was an advance directive on file somewhere. But in truth, knowing Grant, knowing who he was, knowing how active and hands-on he was, there was no need to look at an advance directive. Everyone knew. We knew how he wanted to live. But then, it can't be denied that we all thought to ourselves, what about us? What about our lives without him? The duality of having to let go when you're not ready to let go. The inner, silent fight between what you want to happen and what you know needs to happen. We had reached a crossroads in our grief journey.

Refusal.

Resistance.

Compliance.

And then courage.

Someone brave at the conference room table asked the doctor what would happen when the ventilator was removed. She said that he might die within minutes, or he might live for several weeks longer, depending on the strength of his body. Grant was a big, strong man, and he would probably live for a while, but we couldn't know. It was so strange to think that he was, otherwise, a healthy man. The blockage had now been removed from his artery, and his heart was pumping as it should be. All his other organs were working as they should be. He had color in his skin. If you didn't know otherwise, you'd think he was sleeping.

But he was not there?

The doctor told us to let her know if we had any further questions and then excused herself.

Later that afternoon, all life support was removed. We stood around him, with more prayers. He continued to breathe on his own. But still, he did not wake up. He was then moved out of the cardiac unit and to a different floor and a room that was larger and more comfortable for visitors.

When we had first gathered in Spokane, our focus had been on Grant living. Now that we knew he was dying, our focus changed, necessarily so. The unit mobilized again; we all had a role to play on this grief journey, and we each took a different part.

Bright, shiny light.

We stayed with Grant, all together for the next several days, and in doing so, each began to play our part. Grant's children began to plan details for the funeral. Tim and Grant's other brother, Mike, began writing the obituary, and my sister-in-law wrangled all the younger kids — keeping them fed and busy. Grant's wife began making plans for what to do with his things. I don't know where it came from or why, but I raised my hand and volunteered to write and read the eulogy.[3] And Tim started making plans for what to do with his horses. We were all doing our work — our grief work.

Grant passed six days later, on September 11, 2015. Tim went back to Spokane that weekend with the horse trailer and brought back three mules and two horses.

Yes, it turned out we would need those four loads of hay after all.

One week following Grant's death, we all reunited in Spokane for the funeral. And this time, there were

---

3. Grant's eulogy can be read at www.jennifermelliott.com /grants-eulogy.

even more family and friends who gathered. The service was beautiful.

At the reception after the funeral service, as we circulated and sat and ate a meal with all the visiting family and friends, it was difficult not to notice something quite profound about those who were just comprehending Grant's passing. Those who had been unable to visit him in the hospital, those who hadn't even been aware that he had had a heart attack two and a half weeks earlier, those who had learned after the fact that Grant had died — they were all trailing behind those of us who had been a part of the grief journey from the onset.

We were further down the road in our journeys.

Grief is never a race, and it cannot be rushed. Grief is work, and it is a path that must be traveled. It was through this experience that I learned that there are no shortcuts or fastest routes. However, the earlier you participate in the loved one's dying process, the sooner you begin the journey.

Several weeks later, Grant visited me in a dream. Our family was there, and so were his kids and their families and Grandma Pat. Appropriately, we were outside at a lake. Some of the family was sitting on the beach, while I was in the water, which was shallow for a long way out. I was facing out to the lake when I turned around to look at the beach and saw Grant was in the water halfway between me and the beach. Dressed in his cowboy hat, a T-shirt, and shorts, he was wading out to me. He stopped when I turned around. His hands were touching the water at his sides.

I smiled when I saw him. He smiled back.

"How's Timmy?" he asked.

I didn't answer him. He knew. He had given us some time to prepare for his death. We had known it was coming, yet it was still a huge blow and his vigorous presence was still gone. We weren't OK. I knew it was hard for him to ask the question, and he didn't require me to provide an answer.

But I was so grateful that he was there. He was checking in on us. He was checking in on Tim. There was a warmth and a certainty in his presence. And in that awareness, there was that loving, cozy feeling you get when you are surrounded by your family and everyone is enjoying themselves on a sunny summer day by the lake.

Wherever such dreams come from, and however they happen, there is great comfort to be found in them. The overwhelming sense of goneness you have on a grief journey is replaced by the reassurance of your lost loved one's presence, even if only for a glimmer or moment.

Something happened one day, six years after Grant's passing. Although it was an ordinary Monday morning, during which I had picked up our dog from the groomer, I had this weird feeling driving home, as if it wasn't going to be ordinary. Be careful the thoughts you put out there.

I was in our ranch truck, which we call Old Scratchy. We use it for hauling horses and tools, going to the dump, occasional camping, and taking the dog back and forth to the groomer. The truck is so filthy dirty, I make a point *not* to shower or change if I know I am going to drive it. And yet, that is what makes it so great. I wouldn't want a new truck, because then we'd have to keep it clean. As it happened, the bed was loaded with tools, a ladder, and extension cords that Tim had just picked up from a remodel.

On my way home from the groomer, I was on Colby Road, in the curves. A herd of deer was just starting across the road. I slowed and flashed my lights at the oncoming cars. One yearling, the last one, almost made it over the fence, only to get its back leg caught in the wire fence. It fell to the ground with one leg still caught. Oh no. The more the yearling struggled, the more the wires tightened.

Though I didn't have a plan, I pulled over and put on

the hazard lights. It was so upsetting. No sooner had I pulled over than, from the pasture that the herd of deer had just hastily vacated, three German shepherds came upon the flailing deer.

The poor deer. It began bleating. I began screaming. "Knock it off," I shouted, as though the dogs cared and it would make any difference. *Animal Planet: Predator vs. Prey, Rural Edition*, live streaming.

I found a rock on the ground, thinking, *I'm going to throw this rock at those dogs to get them to stop biting at this poor deer.* And then I thought, *Will it even help? What happens if I hurt the dogs? They are only doing what instinct is telling them to do. It is not their fault this deer has become their prey and I just happen to be standing here all upset and righteous.* But the deer kept bleating. I had never heard one making so much noise.

So, I decided I shouldn't throw a rock at the dogs. But I couldn't let them kill this deer through the fence, and it looked like they might be able to do that. I headed back to the truck and found a hacksaw. (Note that this is all happened in thirty seconds or less).

What a sight that must have been. A beat-up red double-cab with its hazards on. A scruffy-dressed woman, holding back tears, standing next to it with a hacksaw in one hand and a rock in the other, yelling at three dogs doing their best to attack a deer snagged on a fence.

83

At that moment, a big dually truck pulled up right in front of my truck and put his hazards on. A Subaru heading west pulled in right in front of that truck. The gentleman from the truck got out—he tried to free the deer with his hands but to no avail. The gentleman from the Subaru said, "Wire cutters."

Meanwhile, I was just standing there watching—grateful. Somehow, out of nowhere, the owner of the three German shepherds made her way over. She had to literally sit on one of the dogs, pinching its ears to control it.

Both men went back to their vehicles and pulled out wire cutters. Who just carries wire cutters in their vehicles? *Both of them* had wire cutters. Was this a thing? Was this normal, and I just didn't know it? Hacksaws, of course. Wire cutters? I guess, yes.

And they freed the deer. Just like that. The yearling trotted off to find its herd. "Thank you!" I shouted. "Thank you!" the owner of the German shepherds shouted. And off went those wire-cutting, deer-saving heroes, as if it had been nothing. Just all in a day's work, I guess. The take-home message: carry wire cutters in your car—you never know when you might need them.

I got back in the truck and continued my drive home. That experience made me think of Grant. He loved animals, and animals loved him. And it would have been just like him to carry wire cutters everywhere. I just knew he would have done exactly the same thing as those men, had he found himself in the same scenario. And just like them, he would have been a wire-cutting, deer-saving hero.

I had reached the stage where that moment of sadness had a warmer tinge.

Chapter 10

Jerry

48 years old

Jerry Burns became my mom's significant other not long after I got married. She was fifty-eight. I was visiting her one Easter, and he came to the door with a gift bag full of treats and a lovely, pastel-colored blanket. My mom wasn't home at the time, so I received the gift on her behalf. Jerry was a large man with a big barrel of a chest. He had gray hair slicked to the side and was wearing a faded shirt, worn-in cargo shorts, and hiking boots. When my mom arrived back home, I showed her the gift.

"Who was that?" I asked my mom.

"Oh, that's Jerry Burns. He's a neighbor who lives up the road around the bend. His house is the sister to my house. They were both designed by the same architect and look very similar."

Their homes both had white plaster on the outside, along with freethinking clinker brick and local rocks adventurously scattered throughout. You could tell they shared the same architect and builder, with the bricks and rocks being their signature.

"He is so friendly," I said to my mom. I found it interesting that he would give her a blanket. Evocative. A blanket is personal and intimate. To receive a blanket as a gift is a metaphor for a warm, loving hug.

They began dating soon after. And not long after that, he moved in with my mom and sold his childhood home up the road around the bend.

With several generations of family dating back to 1887 having lived in Placer County, Jerry had deep roots there. He had attended Placer High School and would tell stories — shenanigans, really — of all the trouble he and his brother, Sonny, had gotten into. One time he told the story of how, when he was a senior, he had driven his jeep up the front steps of the high school. "You could never do that now — you'd get in so much trouble," he said, laughing. He said this as though lamenting the fact that you wouldn't be able to do that now.

Burns, as he was often called by his close friends, was all about Auburn, Placer County, California, and America, for that matter. He loved the wilderness, the big snow in the mountains, hunting, fishing, and panning for gold. Taking our young kids to the mines was Jerry in his element — outdoors, mines, the Mother Lode, and young kids. He loved kids mostly because he was still a kid himself. Our son's fondest memories of him are built on their shared love of trains: building the train set, watching the trains, and going to the train museum. I honestly don't know who enjoyed it more.

He and my mom had a wonderfully symbiotic relationship in that she loved to cook and Jerry loved to eat. She would give him a shopping list, and he would go to the store. Then she would cook the food, and he would eat it. They both knew they had a good thing going. The special recipe that Jerry would contribute was his homemade ice cream. He had a hand-crank machine that was an antique but worked just the same. He was clearly disappointed in me when he heard I had purchased the plug-in electric type, which he saw as a cop-out. Despite this, making homemade ice cream on all birthdays and the Fourth of July, as Jerry did, became our family tradition.

He was an undergraduate at UC Berkeley and received a Doctor of Pharmacy from the University of Southern California. As he loved watching sports, this always created a conflict in him about which college team to root for when they played each other. Cal or the Trojans? It irritated him that, in professional sports, players would get traded or switch teams.

"It's too bad," he would say. "It's all about the money these days."

This comment was typical of his sincere belief in taking pride and being loyal.

Mom and Jerry frequently traveled together. They visited Guatemala, Ireland, Thailand, Sri Lanka, and all over California and the Pacific Northwest. One of them would have the idea to go, sometimes joining or visiting friends, and the other would agree. And it had become routine for them to head to Hilo, Hawai'i, for the cold months of November, December, and January. They would rent a little house and enjoy the warm, balmy tropical weather for those few months every year.

In April of Jerry's eighty-sixth year, he had a hip replacement. While he hadn't been in pain, he had been unable to walk. Since he'd been a highly active person all his life and in good health, it made sense for him to have this operation. But in doing so, he contracted several infections, which caused him to be in and out of the hospital several times and on several different antibiotics, none of which were working.

I was down for a visit in early July. Jerry looked drawn and thin, markedly different from how he had looked when I had seen him earlier in the spring. My mom was not herself. Being a full-time caregiver was all-consuming, and she was clearly stressed and distracted. And Jerry wasn't eating as he once had. His appetite had diminished. This was deeply concerning to my mom, whose job it was to feed him. But as often happens in such cases, in the months to follow, he seemed to rebound. His strength returned. They even made the long trip up to Bend for a visit.

In October, I went down to see them again, as they were still planning to go to Hawai'i for the yearly snowbird trip. The doctor had given them the go-ahead, and Jerry wanted to go. With the help of the airline and wheelchair assistance, my mom was game to make it all happen.

And so, they went. Everything was fine and easy for the first three weeks of the vacation, and then, while taking a shower, Jerry fell. He was taken to the hospital. One thing led to the next. I was on the phone with my mom two to three times daily with updates. Our daughter and I were already scheduled to fly over for a visit in early December.

In the days that followed his fall, I was working around the house and making to-do lists. I found myself completely unproductive, distracted, lacking focus, and unable to complete easy tasks. I was worried about Jerry's declining health. I was worried about my mom. It became clear to me that the only thing that was going to give me peace of mind was to get on the plane to be with them. I changed our tickets to leave the next morning, and soon after, she called and told me that Jerry had been admitted to hospice. He was septic, and his organs were failing.

The plane landed on the Big Island of Hawai'i in the early afternoon. The warm, balmy air felt the opposite of the cold high desert. The smell of salt and jasmine flowers filled the air. Normally, this would have sent a shot of dopamine through my system, but the hovering sadness held it at bay. We went straight away to Hilo Hospice House. When I walked into the room, Jerry was in the wheeled bed outside on the patio. The clouds had broken, and the sun was peeking through. The birds were singing. I remember thinking how appropriate for him to be outside. I hadn't been sure how I would feel, but I now felt more relaxed, simply being there with them.

The nurses rolled him back inside, and I said hello. His eyes were closed, and though he was nonverbal, with a grunt, he acknowledged I was there. I spoke to him for a bit and then shared a funny video of my husband and our son's recent hunting trip. As I played the video for him, I narrated what was happening. I was laughing as I was telling the story, and Jerry was laughing along — still with his eyes closed. He was conscious yet unconscious. He was with me, yet not there. The best way I can describe it was that he was straddling realms.

My mom had told me that in the days before, he had had a chance to talk to his children, family, and close friends — to say goodbye. After being there for several hours, I had had several conversations with the nurses.

One had been a nurse at the hospital for many years and had moved to Hilo Hospice House three years earlier. I asked her if there was anything she had noticed or learned about from being a hospice nurse. What had she learned about death or impending death?

She promptly answered that there were two things she noticed. The first was that at this particular hospice, at that time, 85 percent of the patients died alone. To be clear, they didn't die without the support of family or friends or the hospice staff—however, they did die when no one else was in the room. That seemed a significant percentage. This was both enlightening and profound. My close girlfriend had told me a story from when her mom was dying of pancreatic cancer. The last three months had been incredibly difficult. One morning, my friend went outside to make a quick phone call on the front porch and when she returned, found her mom had passed.

The hospice nurse prefaced the second observation by saying, "The second thing has happened just too many times not to notice." She said that she would go into a patient's room to check on them, bring them food, or help them with a bathroom break. The room would be empty except for the patient, but the patient would ask, "What are all these people doing here?"

The nurse said that sometimes the patient would comment about a person who had already died, their mother or father, a family member or friend. But the patient had just seen them in the room — sometimes among numerous others. Later, my mom told me that, a day or two before I arrived, Jerry had let out the name Sonny, his brother who had passed many years earlier from cancer.

●

Incidentally, our first child was overdue. (We didn't know if it was a boy or a girl at that time. We chose to be surprised.) Because of my maternity leave, accumulated sick days, and the school schedule, it worked in my favor that the baby was late; this would give me another week with the baby.

I asked the OBGYN, "Who decides when the baby is born? Does the baby decide or the momma decide? Or God, or the Universal Intelligence?"

She laughed. "Ha. If you had the answer to that, you'd be a millionaire." Then she added, "And it would make everyone's life so much easier."

Strangely, as the time passed in this state of limbo, it felt much like birth. It felt much like the same as waiting between the contractions of labor.

It can't be hurried. It can't be slowed.

It just is.

Jerry

My mom and I were sitting on the couch next to Jerry's bed. We were chitchatting. Seems odd to say chitchatting when someone in the room is dying.

Him: Quiescent. Idling. Slumbering.

In truth, I like to believe it gave Jerry comfort knowing I was there with my mom, and chitchatting was the right thing to do, both for her and him. A short time later, the hospice nurse came in and began listening to his fading heartbeat with the stethoscope.

"He is getting close," she said. I was surprised. I wasn't ready to hear this — it seemed so soon. I had only been there for a few hours and was thinking we'd have a few more days with him.

My mom and I immediately jumped to our feet, moving to stand, one on each side of him. His breath slowed. There were long pauses between each one, and then there were no more.

And then something completely unexpected happened. The room filled with what I can only describe as unbounded joy, dynamic and alive — completely overflowing. It felt expansive and buoyant.

It felt consecrated.

It was Jerry. He was everywhere.

I had never been in the presence of a human when they died. I felt so grateful to be there. I felt honored and humbled. Momentous. It was like a gift that I can't explain. And yet, what I hadn't anticipated was the tremendous depth of grief that soon followed.

We would have left to fly back home immediately, but there were things to attend to in the days to follow. Our return flight was scheduled for five days later. The experience was surreal. We would go to the funeral home, followed by a hike to the waterfalls. We would make phone calls regarding how best to bring home his remains, followed by heading to the beach and then out for dinner — enjoying macadamia nut-encrusted fish. It was confusing. Someone in our family had just died. And yet, here we were in this beautiful tropical place. *Should we* embrace it? Or: *We should* embrace it. I decided in this confusion that the words *grief* and *should* make bad bedmates. There shouldn't be any *should*s in relation to grief.

I began asking the question "What feels right in this moment?" because all we can deal with right now is *right now.*

It was decided that Jerry's children would have a memorial for him on what would have been his eighty-seventh birthday, January 21. Meanwhile, we would put Mom on a plane back to California, where my brother would pick her up at the airport. Annie and I would fly back to Oregon for Christmas. It wasn't until we got on the plane that I realized how much I had been holding things together for my mom. I cried for the entire six-and-a-half-hour flight back to Seattle.

The flight attendants somehow knew why.

I don't remember much about Christmas that year. It wouldn't stop snowing for two weeks straight, and upward of three to four feet accumulated, so we were housebound. The grief came in waves, big waves. I would be fine for a couple of days and then sob for hours at a time. Our kids were young teenagers at the time, and I noticed they would do something when they needed a break from the outside world. They would put on their headphones and listen to music. Since we couldn't go anywhere anyhow, I decided to give this a try. I put on music with my headphones and then did something that required little thinking. I took down Christmas decorations and organized all the ornaments. I cried. I vacuumed. I ironed. I cried.

For Christmas, Tim gave me a lovely scented candle. I lit the candle and reorganized and folded clothes in the closet.

Beethoven, Bach, Coldplay, Rush, Annie Lennox, Pharrell — all helped me grieve.

In January, I traveled down to Auburn for Jerry's memorial service. His children had planned it, and it couldn't have been more perfect — down to the very last detail. In the art gallery of the building Jerry owned, they hung large pictures of him, beginning with his baby pictures all the way up to a recent picture of my mom and him walking under the hedges in Northern Ireland. Some of his favorite belongings were sprinkled about — his fishing gear and a tackle box from his cabin. They filled his yellow enamel baby bathtub, now vintage, with tiny bottles of Seagram and 7Up, to make Jerry's drink of choice. For luncheon, they served his favorite lasagna, and of course, there was an ice cream sundae bar, that being his favorite.

His memorial was an important bookend, but I was still early in my grief journey.

A few months later, our family took a trip to Quintana Roo, Mexico. The resort was on the ocean but also featured a pool overlooking a lagoon. I found all I wanted to do was stare at water, either the ocean or the lagoon. Most of the time I had my headphones on, listening to music, looking over the tops of my toes at the water.

Adele, Dvorak, Queen, Led Zeppelin, Haydn, Beck, Sia. I still have the playlist, and they helped me grieve too.

I was tired.

Mentally. Emotionally. Physically.

Grief is depleting.

Rest. Music. Nature. Surrounded and supported by people who love you. Vitamin D from the sun.

Those heal.

It seems appropriate to share Jerry's homemade ice cream recipe. You can also find it online at www.jennifer melliott.com/jerrys-ice-cream-recipe.

Burns's Homemade Ice Cream

Cook Time: ~45 minutes to 1 hour (depending upon the ice cream maker)

Prep Time: 15 minutes

INGREDIENTS
For the Ice Cream:
    3 whole eggs
    1 ⅓ cups white sugar
    2 cups heavy cream
    1 quart half-and-half
    2 teaspoons vanilla
For the Equipment:
    2—3 cups ice cream salt
    several pounds of ice

EQUIPMENT
Ice cream maker/freezer, electric or the old-fashioned hand-crank type

DIRECTIONS

1. Mix ice cream ingredients together by hand for 4 minutes.
2. Pour ingredients into the ice cream maker/freezer.
3. Fill equipment basin with ice and salt.
4. Run mixture until the ice cream is the consistency desired (approx. 45 minutes to 1 hour). Continue to refresh salt and ice as needed.
5. Remove beater and serve immediately.
6. Freeze leftovers.

Chapter 11

Lisa

50 years old

I sent this email to my good friend Lisa the month after Jerry died.

From: Jen Elliott < ███████████████████████ >

Sent: Monday, January 16, 2017 9:20 PM

To: ███████████████

Subject: An update from Bend...

Hi Lisa,

I am thinking of you always. No doubt you've been experiencing an interesting winter in Eugene. We've had crazy snow here in Bend. Tomorrow, the kids will have their eighth snow day/safety day (due to heavy/damaging snow on roofs). Annie and I went to Hawaii to visit my mom and her husband in early December, where they were wintering. My mom's husband (he was 86) fell around Thanksgiving and due to complications, passed away during our visit. I was so grateful to be there with my mom and we helped her pack and return to California. In early January, I accompanied my mother-in-law to OHSU for a week—for a routine diagnostic procedure. Thankfully all went well and we received good news. It has been an interesting six weeks, not to mention the winter we are having.

Meanwhile, back at the ranch—this is how we're doing and I'm hoping it will make you laugh—it is sort of funny when I reflect on it.

Annie: She has attended six of the required 20 days of school (six of 43 calendar days) since Dec. 5th; this is due to our time in Hawaii, Winter Break, and/or snow/safety days. When I announced that school was canceled tomorrow, she shouted (quite exasperated), "MOM, I NEED STRUCTURE AGAIN." To give you context, about 6 months ago, her dad gave her financial incentive to memorize "Paul Revere's Ride" by Henry Wadsworth Longfellow (all 16 paragraphs) in its entirety. She presented it to us tonight. (It was awesome by the way). This is how she has been busying herself.

Michael: He is handling it the best of all of us. Last Tuesday (a snow day delivered to him by God himself with a big red bow) he spent several hours finishing a three-page report about Somalia's Government due in his Honors World History class on Thursday. Not sure when he was planning to finish it WITHOUT the snow day—(ahem). I didn't ask. So—he's been a bit more academically stimulated than his sister as of late.

Tim: Remember this is the man who has asked me previously if I would move to Alaska. Today, when I arrived at the office, he asked me 'IS IT MELTING? Is the temperature above 32 degrees? When is **the** thaw?' Then he repeated this on an hourly basis. I continually remind him that this was why we DIDN'T move to Tahoe to settle 24 years ago.

Thule Dog: Every morning he gets up and looks at Tim as if to ask, "Can we go play now?" "Can I run and run and run, and chase the squirrels and dig for gophers?" And Tim says, "Oh Thule, winter is not your time." Thankfully there is occasionally a jack-rabbit running in the snow that reminds him what his purpose is. Otherwise, he is sleeping a lot, getting a bit wide in the middle like the rest of us, and occasionally catching entertainment from the cats.

The cats: They are fighting more than usual due to the close quarters and their thwarted outdoor time. It is clear that they are especially put out by the cold temperatures and are holding all the humans personally responsible for this inconvenience. Fraidy lives upstairs and Chessie lives downstairs, but they have to cross paths occasionally due to the food and cat box locations. This creates excitement for all of us (especially the dog).

Me: Well thanks be to God I was able to go to Portland at the beginning of January to see green on the ground. And I was looking forward to seeing more green on the ground this weekend in California (for my stepdad's memorial) until I looked at the weather report in Auburn only to find there will be (!@#$$%%^&*-ing) snow in Auburn on Saturday. Are you kidding me? All right then—I've created a sort of twisted challenge for myself—let's see if I can complete ALL of my 2016 tax preparation BEFORE the snow melts. I'm not really sure if this is a win/win or win/lose—or really—what to hope for at this point.

Needless it's not really THAT boring in a boring sort of way. I hope this makes you smile. :)

Love you—

J

I love baseball. I love the sport because:

- Every time I watch a game, I learn something new. The rules, often peculiar, seem endless.
- It's embedded in our American culture. I feel like I'm connected to something bigger. The diversity of players is so great, and they have these side characters who add even more flavor to that already delicious stew that is the game of baseball.

I play a game with my family. I play it more with myself, though, because, usually, no one else is listening. (Not that I can blame them.) I call the game Beyond Baseball—Alternate Profession Profiling. Based on the player's look and affect, I hypothesize: if this player weren't playing baseball, he would probably be...and I brainstorm all the possible professions that he might otherwise undertake. Sometimes I'll include an umpire, a base coach, or a manager, but mostly it's the players. Here are some of the alternate professions that I have imagined:

Electrician
Marketing executive
Work-from-home computer geek

Rap star
High school history teacher who coaches extra-
    duty football
Actor
Lead singer in a rock band
Stand-in for Jesus

I think I'm hilarious. My family thinks I'm a dork, and my husband continually reminds me, "Honey, they're Major League Baseball players. They don't need to consider any other profession." Apparently, this is one of the rare occasions he does take me seriously.

I also love baseball because it is one of those sports where you watch the game intently for forty-five minutes and nothing happens. The score doesn't change. But then you look away for two seconds to grab your water bottle under your seat and miss the winning play (I speak from experience).

The other reason I really enjoy baseball is the fact that it's the only untimed sport.[4] When I attend an MLB game, it is one of the few times in my life that I don't think about the past. I don't think about the future. I don't look at my phone (except to take a picture or look

---

4. Until the 2023 season, when the pitch clock was introduced. But up to that point, Major League Baseball was the only sport untimed in any fashion, and it's still the closest thing we have to that.

up one of those peculiar rules). When I am at an MLB game, I am present. I live in the now.

Eckhart Tolle would approve.

In high school, I dated a shortstop. But much later in my life, it was Lisa who introduced me to the game. I would visit her at her house. She would put on her Giants T-shirt and sit in her big green chair, then pull out the paper and read the stats. Then the game would start, and your choice was to join her or to entertain yourself, and she couldn't have cared less which you chose.

On a business trip together in Denver, we watched a live MLB Rockies game; that was when I got hooked.

I met Lisa when I began teaching a reading program of which she was a coauthor. We became fast friends. She was one of those friends I felt I had known for a lifetime. She was really smart. And sage. We could talk and debate for hours about best practices for reading instruction, argue about politics, toss ideas around about religion, and get lost in pop culture. (In The Lord of the Rings trilogy, she thought Samwise Gamgee was the real hero, not Frodo.) We were open-minded about each other's opinions and valued them. She had many nuggets of wisdom to share. She always encouraged me to do anything I could to reduce the stress in my life. She understood the damage it did to your health.

Lisa was seventeen years my senior, and she lived alone. She had black hair with tight curls and a contagious laugh. Fiscally shrewd, she was a master at living with less.

Simplicity. Inspiring simplicity.

And she loved good coffee. I remember one morning after staying the night at her house I opened the cabinet to get a coffee mug. There were six mugs neatly arranged on the shelf.

She embodied low-impact living. Have what you need. Need what you have. No more, no less. Whether intentional or not, she lived by this mantra. I loved being in her space for this reason.

When I was with Lisa, I knew I could tell her anything — and it would always stay with her. Not that I had much to divulge, but I felt safe. She was a true confidante. I could ask her anything, and I knew I wouldn't be judged. And she would speak the truth.

●

In early December 2016, I got a call from a mutual colleague who said that Lisa had a rare form of lung cancer. They would be trying several types of therapy to see if they could slow the growth. I burst into tears. I thought about her and how, more than anything, she loved her son and her young grandchildren. I thought about them and how lucky they were to call her mom and grandma. They were her greatest joy. I felt so sad. And selfishly, I panicked. In my life, she was such a big fencepost that I could lean on and the wall that I bounced ideas off. Both were going to disappear. There was no one else like her in my life: a colleague and peer who challenged and supported me in my professional life as well as my personal life, and in that space where they often blended. As she was also a mother, teacher, consultant, and elder, she was a dear friend who also understood me from a place of experience. We had a unique relationship.

In the year and a half that followed, I spoke to her on the phone several times. I kept offering to come over to see her. I offered to stay in a hotel so as not to cause her more work. I just wanted to see her. She never responded to my overtures. I think she felt uncomfortable about her changing appearance; she did say some things to that effect.

Lisa told me a story that I think about often. She had gone to lunch with a couple of girlfriends. They were talking about the remodeling projects they were working on for their house — the new tile they were installing and the colors of paint they were choosing for their walls. She told me that, when you are dying of a terminal illness, such things as new tiles for the bathroom and paint colors for the walls are no longer of significance, and she found she had little in common to talk about with these friends. Her priorities had changed. She didn't really specify the priorities, but it was implicit: family, friendships, meaningful relationships, love — and time (remaining). These transcended.

I think about this conversation a lot.

I wanted to see her. I wanted to be a part of her life as she was experiencing this illness. Not knowing what else to do, I regularly sent her emails and cards, and hand creams. I imagined that the chemo was making her skin dry. I wrestled with how to stay close to her while not being able to see her.

Then a song found me. At that time, music streaming services were not available and the local radio stations were barren. I splurged on a membership to SiriusXM, a satellite radio service, and it was one of the first songs I heard through it, as I was thinking about Lisa. "People Get Ready," written by Curtis Mayfield, played by Rod Stewart and Jeff Beck. It has been covered by multiple artists since The Impressions originally sang it.

The song was written in the 1960s, during the civil rights movement, and online sources confirm that it speaks to grit, tenacity, liberation, and redemption.

Courage. Strength. Hope.

For me, it's also about death, but in the same way. Courage. Strength. Hope.

It's about being emancipated from all earthly materialism.

No need for tiles or new paint.

No baggage. No emotional baggage. Leave it all behind.

In the end, all that matters is love.

As I drove, I would listen to this song. And I would think of Lisa. I would think of her boarding the train. I would think of myself boarding the train.

Lisa died in late May 2018. I miss her. I miss her a lot.

I am so glad I have a song that reminds me of her.

And I never walk into a ballpark without thinking of Lisa. This would make her very happy.

I still love baseball.

I love the game because...Lisa.

Chapter 12

Frances

52 years old

It was early October, two and half months since we had finished and moved into the remodel of our first Bend house, the cute little craftsman behind the Westside Bakery in downtown Bend. After church, Bill Barnes, an old friend of the family, approached Tim. Bill had been appointed the executor of the estate of his next-door neighbor, who had recently passed, and was selling the house on the estate's behalf. Was Tim interested in taking a look before it hit the market?

Over breakfast, Tim timidly mentioned this to me.

"You're crazy," I said. "We *just* moved into this remodel."

"I'm going to see it today," he said.

He came home later that afternoon. "I think you'd better go look at that house," he said. He knows me well and knew I'd like it.

"OK...but we're still unpacking boxes," I said, but reluctantly I agreed.

The house on Dove Tail Road was 1,328 square feet. The remodel downtown by the bakery had three bedrooms; this house had two. The remodel had one bathroom; this house had two. The remodel had an unusable detached garage, good for parking a lawn mower; this house had a two-and-a-half-car garage. The remodel sat on a postage stamp — but you could walk downtown, which was nice; this house had half an acre. The remodel, originally built in 1929, had basically no storage, not even a dedicated laundry space; this house not only had a laundry room but abundant closets and storage. I have since grown to learn that the most important word in this paragraph is *storage*. It doesn't matter the size of your house or the size of the rooms — as long as you have *storage*.

If we were to buy it, I did have one request. "Can I convert the stove from electric to gas? It only needs to be piped fourteen feet."

"Done," Tim agreed.

We sold the house downtown and moved into the new house — just in time to set up a Christmas tree. Bill and his wife, Frances, were our next-door neighbors.

There were a few updates to complete before we moved in, but they were easy and small compared to the downtown house. We were working on them one weekend when Bill and Frances dropped in to see what we were up to. Bill was confounded that we were replacing the olive-green carpet and the brass light fixture with swooping brass chains. "It's perfectly good carpet; why would you replace it?" he exclaimed.

Frances asked what we were doing in the kitchen.

"We're switching out the electric stove for a gas range," I said. "And then putting down new vinyl."

"Can I do that?" Frances asked Bill.

"No," he bluntly replied.

Frances gave me a side glance with a half-smile.

Over the next couple of years, we spent a lot of time with Bill and Frances. We would go out to breakfast with them after church, or we'd have dinner with them at the golf course where we were all members. I learned a lot about Frances and adored her. She was very tall and lean and athletic. She worked as a PE teacher, which made total sense — she loved the outdoors and was highly active, playing tennis and golf, downhill skiing, hiking, riding horseback, and fishing. She told me that, at one point, she had had five children all under the age of six — in my opinion, this is cape-worthy. And she was a great cook.

When I was pregnant with our first child, I would walk every day for two miles. Sometimes she would walk with me. She said I motivated her, but in fact, she motivated me. A sixty-eight-year-old still golfing, hiking, skiing, and playing tennis. Even though she was always nursing her knee, she still pushed on.

115

Frances told me a story once of how they had been driving their thirty-foot RV to South Dakota to visit family. Bill had been asleep, and she had driven through a heavy snowstorm. I thought she was brave to have done that.

The summer after we moved into the house, I went over to their house to get a recipe of hers and noticed a gas range in the kitchen.

"Is that new?" I asked.

"Not too new," she replied. "It was installed soon after you and Tim moved in next door."

She gave me a wink. Frances possessed an inner knowingness. While it was true that she was very kind, she was also an accurate judge of character; she did not suffer fools but acted on this in such a way that the fools were none the wiser. I always felt there was a storehouse of untapped wisdom within her — she was a hidden treasure or an unturned rock, an undiscovered arsenal of goodness to share.

Frances taught me how to make raspberry jam using wax to seal the jars (the old-fashioned way) and shared the caramel recipe that she made for Christmas. It's so easy — it feels like you're cheating.

Frances possessed a uniquely female power. In thinking about her and the female archetypes, I would check the following boxes: The Mother, The Warrior, and The Sage.

Four years later, soon after our son was born, we moved again, across town. We were busy raising our young family and saw less and less of our old neighbors. In February 2008, Bill and Frances celebrated their fiftieth wedding anniversary. Bill passed away ten months later. Frances was heartbroken without him. Every so often, we would run into Frances around town, usually with one of her kids.

●

A couple of years ago, out of the blue, Frances came to my mind. I thought about her on the golf course, the house on Dove Tail Road with ample storage and the gas range, and going for walks with her when I was thirty-nine weeks pregnant.

I thought, *I should call her and say, "Let's have breakfast together."* Perhaps selfishly on my part, part of my motivation was to learn from her storage of untapped wisdom.

Then I allowed life to get in the way, and I never followed up.

Three months later, I saw her obituary in the local newspaper. My heart ached. Why hadn't I reached out to her when my instinct told me to do so?

If you are missing someone...call them.

If you want to see someone...visit or invite them.

If you love someone...tell them.

Don't wait.

Frances's Caramels

Frances dictated this recipe to me, and I wrote it down. You'll notice it doesn't involve a candy thermometer. If you want to do so, do a Google search on how to use the thermometers; however, I've had good luck just following her description. This recipe can also be found online at www.jennifermelliott.com/Frances-Caramel-Recipe.

Cook Time: Several hours to cool

Prep Time: 25 minutes plus time to harden

INGREDIENTS
1 cup white sugar
½ cup Karo syrup
1 ½ cups heavy cream

EQUIPMENT
Jelly roll pan
Candy thermometer (optional)

Directions
1. Mix sugar, syrup, and ½ cup of cream in a heavy-bottom saucepan over medium heat.
2. Cook until it forms a soft ball.

3. Add another ½ cup of cream.
4. Cook until it forms a soft ball.
5. Add the remaining ½ cup of cream until it forms a hard ball.
6. Pour in a buttered or parchment-lined jelly roll pan.
7. Cool.
8. Cut into squares.
9. Sometimes Frances would wrap the caramels individually in wax paper squares, twisting the ends.

Chapter 13

David

When I taught kindergarten, we were fortunate enough to have educational assistants, sometimes called para pros or instructional assistants, in our school district. They were there to provide additional support for the students and teachers in both general and special education classrooms. When these assistants were absent, they would have a substitute for the day. In my second year of teaching kindergarten, I had a student named Corbin who struggled with behavior, having frequent outbursts. He would scuffle and pick fights with the other students. As a result of this, he had a special education assistant who would drop in during class time to check in with him and help diffuse any flare-ups.

One day, early in the school year, a bald, burly-chested man with large hands walked into our kindergarten classroom. He must have been six foot four, with a commanding presence that filled the room. When this happened, I, along with the twenty-five or so five-year-olds, stopped and looked his way. Compared to the five-year-olds, who were of course small in stature, along with the accompanying small chairs and tables, this stout human in our midst seemed a giant. One of the students asked, "Is he our new principal?" A fair question indeed, I thought. This was before staff were required to wear name badges.

We introduced ourselves. He was Mr. Blahnik, a substitute special educational assistant here for the day, and it was his time to check in with Corbin. I introduced Mr. B. to the class, and everyone sat up a little straighter in their seats. They didn't even know why they were doing it, but they did. I made note. I showed Mr. B. to the table where he would be sitting but brought over one of the few adult chairs in the classroom so that his knees wouldn't hit his chin. Corbin was delighted. They chatted as Corbin worked. I remember Mr. B.'s enormous fingers pinching a crayon and coloring along with Corbin and the other students sitting at the table. His gentle, benign presence in the classroom had a calming effect. While I would like to think of myself as having good classroom management, I appreciated the extra layer of resolve I felt when he was in the room.

I soon learned that David Blahnik was a retired lieutenant colonel in the US Army, after which he had helped build Trident submarines. He still had a love for work and was beginning his third career as a substitute educational assistant. Amazing. And while it now all made sense, and I loved it when he was in the classroom, he remained an enigma. I knew there was more to this man.

A year or so later, while looking for a new house with acreage, we scheduled a viewing of what I saw as my dream house. The owners, David and his wife, met us at the door. I was completely surprised. It was so interesting to see him in his home. And it was beautiful. I learned from his wife, Charlene, that during David's military career, they had lived in twenty different countries. David spoke French in addition to learning several other languages and had also earned a master's degree in international relations and public administration.

Charlene was an artist, and between her creations and all the treasures they had collected from their travels, their home was teeming with unique objects, souvenirs, and art. In particular, there were some beautiful pieces from Asia. Their home echoed and retraced their experiences abroad and elegantly wove together the media, textures, and presentations of differing cultures into a delicious melting pot of interior décor. It told a story, and an adventurous one. I not only loved the design of the house but loved the richness of the narrative within it. In addition, the fact that they lived there gave it good vibes. David walked us around the twenty acres — the pump house, the irrigation pond, the green pastures and juniper trees. He had built a bench next to the pond. It was so peaceful.

They were selling the house to downsize.

Oh, I really wanted that house, but it was outside our price range.

"That's my dream house," I complained to our realtor and friend.

He gave me a side glance. "You're too young for your dream house."

I think about that comment often. I think I was twenty-nine or thirty at the time. Do you have to be a certain age to have your dream house? I've since learned that a dream house is sort of a moving target as one ages. What had been my dream house would no longer be a few years later. In hindsight, every house I've lived in has been my dream house in its own way, due to the time we lived there and for the memories it held. (That, and *storage!*)

We didn't buy their house. We didn't even make an offer.

I pouted a bit.

I continued to run into David at school, in my classroom and in the hallways. A couple of years later, we happened to run into him and his wife after church. I hadn't even realized we went to the same one.

Life went on. My profession changed, and I rarely saw them, until one day after church, it was just David.

David

We learned his wife had passed away. He was clearly sad, but as his smiley, warm self, he was also getting on with life.

At the tail end of COVID, once again by reading the obituaries in the paper, I learned of his death. Out of nowhere, or perhaps not out of nowhere but from somewhere deep down, I began crying. Why was I crying? I had known David, but not well. He had worked in my classroom some twenty-four years earlier, but not often. I had been in his house, but only once. Our paths had crossed, but only rarely. Why was I crying?

I went to his funeral. I signed the guest book and wondered if the family would see my name and ponder who this stranger was at their father's funeral. Guest books are an interesting thing. Does the family look at them? Or if it's a wedding, do the bride and groom look at them? They serve a purpose, since both events, weddings and funerals, tend to be so full of emotion that somehow our memories are wiped clean. Even if it's a happy event like a wedding, we don't remember it well. Guest books serve as documentation of who attended.

David's son delivered an engaging and detailed eulogy about his dad. And I learned more about this man and his adventurous life.

I am glad I went to his funeral.

I would have liked to have known David better. He would have been a wonderful friend.

Maybe that is why I cried.

●

The old me, the less brave me, the one who wasn't willing to engage in a relationship with grief, would not have gone to David's funeral. I would have created some excuse or reason why I didn't need to go, how our paths rarely crossed anymore and we didn't know each other very well anyway. But if you're reading between the lines, what the old me really would have been saying was *denial*.

But now I know better.

I went to David's funeral with intention. I listened, I sang, I prayed. I was reminded how our actions count. I reflected on David's impact, which, in turn, made me consider my own. I spent time in a community with other people who were grieving his death. And while my journey was likely a shorter experience than many of theirs would be, I said goodbye. I participated.

We attend funerals to honor the person who has died, but there is another layer too: in doing so, we also honor ourselves.

The Takeaways

My husband and I each have our own cell phones, of course. Each has a list of contacts, photos, social media apps, streaming services, and email platforms, to name just a few. Some of our contacts cross over, but mostly, our phones and emails contain entirely distinctive contacts and topics that align with our professions. Our searches, interests, and sensibilities have carefully honed our social media and news so that our feeds are different. We enjoy many of the same songs and pieces of music, but our playlists are individual. We travel together, so our photos are of the same locations, and frequently of our children, but our perspectives vary. And, of course, most of my pictures include him, and most of his pictures include me. Our selfies with each other vary slightly, depending on who takes them. Because my husband and I share a life together, the content overlaps. Much of the content of our phones interestingly forms a characterization, a biography almost, of our life together. However, by virtue of our individual experiences, they diverge and are all their own unique.

And so it is with each death experience and the grief process that follows. Some of the qualities may be similar for all the people affected by it. Some will overlap. But it will be different every time and for every person. Probably my biggest takeaway from these personal accounts is that the process of healing from grief is a journey—a series of sojourn, really, temporary stopovers. The relationship you had with the deceased and where you are in your life at that moment will affect both the energy you have for this journey and the journey itself.

How long does this journey take?

My answer to myself is always this: Like the time-consuming act of driving fifteen miles per hour through a heavy snow- or rainstorm—when your fatigued windshield wipers can barely keep up and you can hardly see—you get there when you get there. Because it will take as long as it takes. And in many instances, the grief will always be there; it doesn't fully go away. But perhaps you will develop a better relationship with the grief over time. This way, you can learn to be in the same room with the grief, rather than closing the door on it, and perhaps even take it by the hand and walk together. In his book *The Five Invitations*, Frank Ostaseski states, "There is no 'right' way to grieve, no timetable, no one path. And there certainly are no shortcuts through grief. The only way is straight through the middle."[5]

But maybe there is a better way to grieve that gives us strength and provides tools for the turbulence ahead. The following are suggestions that have helped me in my grief explorations. Some I did intentionally, but mostly, they were unplanned. Upon reflection, I realized that these activities helped me heal. There is no guarantee that they will help you. But certainly, they are worth trying.

The suggestions don't require resources, not in the financial sense at least, but they do require inner resources — the first one being courage. The next is patience. Grief doesn't come with a date stamp. Acceptance is a big hitter. Yielding is quiet but powerful. And time. Time is potent. Be intentional as you participate. Grief requires your loving kindness and attention. And in return, healing is a form of love.

When possible, and as much as you are comfortable while also practicing courage, be a part of the dying person's experience and their memorial and/ or burial process.

---

5. *Frank Ostaseski, The Five Invitations: Discovering What Death Can Teach Us About Living Fully* (New York: Flatiron Books, 2017), 158.

This suggestion was probably one of the most important and surprising realizations from my grief experiences. At first, I believed this to be counterintuitive. Why would I want to intentionally participate in these activities when they would most certainly be uncomfortable and sad? But in fact, being courageous (there it is again) and opting into things that are not always easy, such as making hospice or hospital visits, helping to write the obituary, delivering the eulogy, picking out the flowers, or attending the funerals, will actually *initiate* the journey down the (inescapable) path of grief. It feels good to be doing something meaningful for this person who had meaning in your life. And typically, you are doing these activities with other loved ones. Grieving and doing something meaningful *with community and in that community* is, in and of itself, healing.

If possible, say goodbye before they die.

Best if you can do this in person. It will be the last time you see this person, and there are many levels of communication, spoken and unspoken, that take place in someone else's presence. The next best option is a phone call or video call. And if these options aren't a possibility, then write a letter. And even if the person (or animal) has passed and you missed the opportunity to say goodbye, you can still write to them and say goodbye. Any kind of closure helps us take the next step.

Carve out time to grieve. Recognize that grief and being a part of a loved one's death experience takes emotional capital, which involves work (struggle), time, and energy (stamina and endurance). Honor this.

Expect it. Affirm it and accept it. It drains, enervates, and exhausts. While you might have only so many days of work leave for bereavement, your grief will be on a different time schedule. Just being aware that the effects may stay with you for a long while, like a stubborn illness, helps. Welcome self-compassion, hold yourself lightly, and try to get a decent amount of sleep. As Matthew Walker, a neurologist and sleep specialist, says in his class on MasterClass®, The Science of Better Sleep, "In some ways, it's not time that heals all wounds — it's time during sleep and, particularly during dream sleep, that provides this emotional convalescence."[6]

Pay attention to music. Listen to it and choose it carefully. Pay attention to the songs that find you.

---

6. Matthew Walker, "Episode 1: What Is Sleep?" MasterClass®, The Science of Better Sleep, 10:32, https://www.masterclass.com/classes/matthew-walker-teaches-the-science-of-better-sleep.

After Jerry died, I crawled into my head with music. Coming through my headphones, the songs allowed me to both escape and connect at the same time. The music enabled me to go deep into my grief, and, as with sleep, the music also smoothed the edges. In other experiences, songs found me. They took me to that person as I held them in mind.[7] When Lisa was dying, Rod Stewart and Jeff Beck's version of Curtis Mayfield's "People Get Ready" found me. When I heard it, it gave me something to hang on to, something to cling to, and it allowed me to connect with her when I wasn't able to see her. After she died, another song found me, "See You Again" by Wiz Khalifa featuring Charlie Puth. The lyrics speak to the friendship we had, and it gave me hope. It still does.[8]

Take part in rote activities.

Rote activities endure a poor reputation. They are considered boring, mundane, and repetitive. However, because of my experiences of grief, I have a whole new

---

7. For more information on this idea, see Benjamin Zander, "The Transformative Power of Classical Music," TED Talks, February 2008, video, 20:13, https://www.ted.com/talks/ben jamin_zander_the_transformative_power_of_classical_music.

8. To see the companion playlist for this book, visit www. jennifermelliott.com/the-playlist.

appreciation for their role in our lives. Examples of rote activities include vacuuming, ironing, raking, laying bricks, leaf blowing, chopping vegetables, doing dishes, digging in the garden, washing the car, and folding clothes. They require physical activity with repetition and typically no decisions with significant consequences. For example, if you are vacuuming, it doesn't matter if you vacuum the bedroom or the kitchen first; if you're working in the kitchen, it doesn't matter if you peel the carrots or the potatoes first or wash the bowl or the pan. It doesn't matter; it just all needs to be done. But something transformative happens in this process. Your brain relaxes, and ideas come — sometimes from that deep place. Solutions present themselves. You're productive. You're in control. Healing occurs when you're not thinking about it.

Make things.

It is also worth exploring creative activities. We are meant to create. You don't have to be a craftsman, an artist, or a professional to participate. Tell your inner perfectionist to take the day off and dig in. Choose something easy. Be a beginner. Bake, draw, build, paint, sand, form, write, code, act, sing, dance, photograph, carve, plant, sew, craft, paste, color, knit, design. Intentionally hold in mind the person or animal you have lost as you create. Again, you're being productive. You're in control. In addition, there is great satisfaction in completion and gratification in making something that wasn't there before.

Spend time outside. Give yourself permission to just stare at and be in nature.

Several months after Jerry died and we were in Mexico, all I wanted to do was stare at the ocean. In February 2021, my cousin unexpectedly passed away. In the spring, his memorial took place outside, on the edge of Lake Tahoe. We were positioned so we could look at the lake during the service. The lake was still, blue, and vast: calming, soothing, and healing.

It needn't be water; it can be trees, the forest, the desert, or mountains. And even in the busiest of cities, you can always find a park or a garden. When we were visiting Dublin last summer, we walked through St. Stephen's Green, a public garden square and park in the city center. As soon as I walked through the gate, I was transported. I no longer saw the buses or the taxis or heard the honking horns or the clamor of city life; instead, I saw trees, ponds, flowers, grass, squirrels, and birds.

Beauty. Quiet. Stillness. Mindfulness. Healing.

Write.

Write longhand if you can, where your hand is physically connected to the page through the pen or pencil. Writing longhand is slower and more tedious, but as a result, the ideas have more time to brew and cultivate. You don't have to write about a certain topic or subject. Don't worry about punctuation or the neatness of your handwriting; just let the words come up and come out. As with rote activities, it seems your brain relaxes when you are doing this. In the process of encoding your words and putting them on the page, thoughts are unpacked. Some of these thoughts are old. But the new ones — have they always been there? Or did the writing create them? I don't know how. I don't know why. I just know that, as with sleeping, writing is another activity that smooths the edges.

Find a productive, meaningful way to carry the memory of the person with you.

This could be done in the way of ritual, some form of remembrance or celebration in honor of that person. It could be making their homemade ice cream recipe and serving it on the Fourth of July. It might be going to baseball games, their favorite sport; participating in the hobby they taught you; or wearing their charm brace-let or belt buckle. You might hang a piece of their art in your house or use the bowl they always filled with cashews on the kitchen counter. It needn't be fancy or expensive, just intentional and meaningful. It is in these rituals or activities that you learn to take grief by the hand and walk with it.

Walk toward grief, not away from it. Hold it. Sit with it. Eventually, it will move on, or at least move further away.

This takes courage. (Yes, more of it.) The pain that accompanies grief is widespread and uncomfortable. It takes courage to be uncomfortable. The goneness aches; it physically aches. Your body is trying to process your emotions, and it is telling you that something is not right. It will do this in a variety of ways. The worst thing you can do is ignore what your body and emotions are telling you; instead, yield to it. Feel your way through it. Feel your way into the ache. Let it out. The ache has to come out. Avoiding suffering will prolong it. If these feelings are repressed and buried, they are likely to manifest in negative ways, such as depression, disease, addiction, sickness, or social withdrawal.

Ask for help.

Reach out for support. This could be from friends, family, professional counselors or therapists, death doulas, chaplains, or grief support groups. And pray. Pray for the person who died. Pray for your own healing.

Be available to others who are grieving.

You needn't even talk; just be with them. And if they do want to talk, listen. Be brave, open, without judgment, and sensitive; be a generous and stable presence in spirit and in fact. Take those extra days if you need to. Work can wait. Being available to support others cannot.

Talk about death.

Talk about it with your parents, your children, your family, and your friends. Learn to get comfortable with it and help them get comfortable with it.

Life is fast; time is short.

Waste no time.

We are all going to die — this, too, will happen to you.

Acknowledgments

I t's true it takes more than a writer to make a book. First and foremost, a heart full of gratitude to all of those who have passed before me, who taught me both in their living and in their dying to be a braver person, to better accept that change is life and if we are open to it and look for it, benevolence can be found.

Death is very personal. I realize what a big ask it was to have people read their loved one's chapter, fact-check, and also give me their blessing to write about them in this book. I am honored you would help me tell my story in this way: Jerry Neft (my dad); Kim Bateman; Missy Scott, Dan Elliott, Cindy McSmith, Carolyn Basque, David Burns; Joanne Neft (my mom); Michael Scott; Kristin Okhuysen and Jay Blahnik. I appreciate you all.

Thank you to Lyla Rothschild at the Ernest Becker Foundation and Kim Bateman for your additional insights and contributions.

I offer my many thanks to Curt Garner, who encouraged me to write this book in a casual conversation that surfaced during a house remodel. Huge gratitude for Geoffrey Berwind, the consummate coach, cheerleader, and sounding board who encouraged, "Keep going," and also, "I think you have more poems in you." Deb Englander, thank you for believing in my writing, and Christina Smith, for holding my feet to the fire. Thank you to the many talents who contributed not only their craft but lots of handholding as well: Laurie Chittenden, Hugh Barker, Vinnie Kinsella, Kristin Thiel, Jason Booher, Mary Guiseffi, and Stephanie Foster. My niece, Missy Scott, was the very first beta reader. You gave me a much-needed second wind. Thank you.

To my dear friends, you know who you are, and my mom, who nudged and kept asking me, "How goes the writing?" To our children, Michael and Annie, always supportive and encouraging, I love you. And to my Tim, who always asks, "What are you making?" and patiently awaits the answer, which might be a collage, a sweater, a painting, a business, a family, a home, cookies, chili, friendships, a song, a poem, a story, and now, a book. Thank you for providing me with time, space, and resources to creatively express myself. After you and our children, it is in making things that I find the greatest joy. I love you.

Recommendations for Further Reading

Written by a grief counselor and bereavement educator, Zen priest and researcher, *Bearing the Unbearable: Love, Loss and the Heartbreaking Path of Grief*, by Dr. Joanne Cacciatore, is organized into fifty stand-alone chapters. The stories and anecdotes are primarily from those who have lost a child. They capture both the pain and the redemption of grief, drawn from patients in Cacciatore's therapy practice and the pain she herself felt in losing her newborn child. Cacciatore captures a variety of facets and angles of grief and the pain of loss and provides excellent suggestions, for example, establishing rituals or micro rituals, practicing self-care, and developing sleep and kindness projects.

Option B: Facing Adversity, Building Resilience and Finding Joy was written by Sheryl Sandberg and Adam Grant. *Option B* combines Sandberg's personal insights with Grant's eye-opening research on finding strength in the face of adversity, beginning with the gut-wrenching moment when Sandberg finds her husband dead of an arrhythmia caused by undiagnosed coronary heart disease. The narrative documents Sandberg's insights and feelings from that moment, through telling their children, planning and attending the funeral, going back to work, and then living as a single mother and thinking of allowing herself happiness and dating again. Grant's suggestions and wisdom to assist Sandberg in her healing are sprinkled throughout; it is part self-help and part memoir.

Crying in H Mart: A Memoir, written by Michelle Zauner, the lead singer of the band Japanese Breakfast, recounts her youth and the story of her sometimes-tumultuous relationship with her mother during adolescence. Raw and authentic in detail, the author recounts learning of her mom's diagnosis of terminal cancer and caring for her, and ultimately her death. The one bond she and her mother shared was their love of both cooking and eating Korean food, a common thread throughout the book. The memoir is lovingly written and descriptive, providing deep insights into how the author thought and felt during the experience of growing up with and losing her mom and the grief associated with her death.

With an abundance of experience, Zen Hospice House cofounder Frank Ostaskeski wrote *The Five Invitations: Discovering What Death Can Teach Us About Living Fully* as an invitation to awaken our awareness of death, which in turn can help us better fully live our lives. The book provides examples, anecdotes, and stories drawn from both his own experience with severe illness and those of patients at Zen Hospice House.

Michael Hebb's *Let's Talk about Death (Over Dinner): An Invitation and Guide to Life's Most Important Conversation* faces head-on the importance of the conversation surrounding death. He addresses both practical considerations such as wills and do not resuscitate options and emotional ones: what we fear and what we hope about our own death and how we want to be remembered. Hebb cofounded the organization Death Over Dinner, which encourages people to meet for dinner, eat, and talk about the one inevitable thing we have in common. In his book, he offers practical advice on how to have these conversations. He shares tested prompts and conversation starters from the spiritual to the practical, sometimes surprising and funny — all to address death with the goal of making our lives more meaningful.

For additional suggested readings, check out www.jennifermelliott.com/resourcese4a228db.

Photo by Gallivan Photo.

About the Author

A writer with a background in education, Jennifer Elliott is, at heart, a teacher. With experiences teaching kindergartners through high school students, presenting and training teachers, and writing curricula, she understands learners coming at topics from diverse mindsets and viewpoints. When not writing or teaching, Jennifer loves to travel, search for treasures in antique stores, watch baseball, and volunteer for hospice. Jennifer lives in Bend, Oregon, with her husband. They have two children, two cats, and one very spoiled golden retriever.

You can find more resources, recommendations, workshops, events, and writing on a host of topics from Jennifer at www.jennifermelliott.com.

Substack: jennifermelliott
Pinterest: jennifermelliottwrites
Instagram: jennifermelliottwrites